MARRIAGE & ME

A

Must-Read

for

Every

Chasan

and

Kallah

ISBN 979-862-644-345-5

Design: Ben Gasner Studio, Jerusalem

MARRIAGE & ME

Step-by-Step Torah Guidance to Transform the Me into a We

Rav Nachum Chaimowitz

Rabbi Yitzchak Berkovits

Sanhedria HaMurchevet 113/27
Jerualem, Israel 97707
02-5813847

הרב יצחק שמואל הלוי ברקוביץ

ראש רשת הכוללים לינת הצדק
סנהדריה המורחבת 113/27
ירושלים ת"ו

בס"ד

ירושלים ת"ו ד' באדר הסמוך לניסן תשע"ט

My friend of many years, Harav Nochum Chaimowitz Shlita, has reached the hearts of talmidim here in Yerushalaim and across the Atlantic, and has offered guidance and support to so many in the most pivotal years of their lives. I have witnessed him lead bochurim to the chupah and, with endless dedication, continue to guide them in building their homes on the basis of Torah and serving Hashem.

Rabbi Chaimowitz has now put years of experience into sound advice in print for the general public. I am sure this work will be well received and will assist many in building healthy, happy marriages.

בברכה,

יצחק ברקוביץ

Rabbi Noach Orlowek
Rechov Sorotzkin 51/2, Jerusalem

הרב נח אורלווייק
רחוב סורוצקין 51/2, ירושלים

בס"ד

ירושלים ת"ו יד ניסן תשע"ט

Rav Nochum Chaimowitz Shlita, is known in Yerushalayim as a dedicated teacher and guide for those embarking on their path in Yahadus, both at the beginning of their path and guiding them through some of the most difficult and fateful decisions of their lives. He has had years of blessed experience in helping people build their homes and make them into sanctuaries of Sholom Bayis. I remember him, with his warm heart and resolute soul, as having inspired young couples to build families that are undreamed of in the hedonistic, material world. He has now put into writing some of his ideas, anchored in our Torah tradition, and spiced with his own words, which emit from a pure and caring heart. May he, and all of us, merit to see the fruits of his labor of love become a reality for many more families; those just beginning their journey and those who have already begun to nurture the Jewish people with vibrant and joyous families that are a credit to our people.

בברכה,

נח אורלווייק

Kehilla Kedosha Ramat Eshkol
Paran St, Jerualem

Rabbi Shmuel Zucker

קהילה קדושה רמת אשכול
רח' פארן, ירושלים

הרב שמואל צוקער
מרא דאתרא

בס"ד
ל' חשוון תש"פ

I have been zoche to have known Rabbi Nachum Chaimowitz Shlita for many years and know that he has been a very successful *mechanech* to all of his students. He guides them by bringing out their individual uniqueness and devotes his time in preparing them for the continuation of their lives in a balanced and healthy way by teaching them to value the importance of Shalom Bayis even before marriage.

All of this was done amidst the deep and heartfelt shiurim that he has given based on the holy teachings of the בעש"ט ותלמידיו – who themselves were well-known for their emphasis on Shalom Bayis as a prerequisite for true and complete Avodas Hashem*.

I am excited to see that much of the remarkable *hadracha* that he has been giving for Shalom Bayis has now been put into writing, enabling a wider circle of couples to benefit from them.

Hashem should grant him אריכות ימים ושנים in good health and he should continue his עבודת הקודש in bringing shalom to so many more Jewish homes.

בידידות נצח,

שמואל יצחק צוקער

---

*Author's note: Such as the Rebbe **Reb Mecheleh of Zlotchov** *zy"a*, who did not get upset at his Rebbetzin for breaking the *pitum* on his invaluable Esrog; the **Apte Rov** *zy"a*, who did not get upset at his Rebbetzin for switching the *shmura* matzos that he was expecting to use on Pesach for *push-uteh* matzos; and the **Kotznitzer Maggid** *zy"a* who incorporated into his own *minhagim* the "*Shulem Bayis Kugel*" - just for the sake of helping other couples to have Shalom Bayis in *their* homes.

In loving memory
and as a merit for
our dear Father

Shlomo Hershel
ben Baruch *a"h*

Married for 52 years to our mother
(May she live and be well)

He was a beautiful example
of Shalom Bayis that we strive to emulate.

נפטר כ"ד אדר א', תשע"ט לפ"ק
ת.נ.צ.ב.ה.

Contents

Preface

Over the years in my capacity as a teacher and *madrich* (*halachic* and spiritual guide), many issues among students and their spouses have arisen which required individual attention. As I would listen to the couples who were going through a myriad of varying issues and would try to help them with advice based upon Torah *hashkafah* (Jewish outlook), it became clear to me that there were certain **rules of Shalom Bayis** that applied to every situation.

What more, it became evident that *if only the couples would have been aware of these rules earlier* – before their disagreements had erupted – they probably would not have reached the extenuating circumstances they were in when they *finally did come* to speak about their issues.

I therefore compiled these rules in a basic way with their Torah sources, and began teaching them to *chasanim* (grooms) in order to prepare them for marriage. The overwhelming majority of *chasanim* have expressed that these rules have been helpful to them. They equipped them with the **practical tools** for continued growth in their Shalom Bayis once they got married.

These rules are especially necessary for every chasan and kallah today, since, unfortunately, it has become common to hear about many newly married couples who find themselves in a relationship *without any clue whatsoever* as to how their marriage "is supposed to be". Starting off with a proper understanding of *what a marriage relationship is supposed to look like,* can help to avoid the very serious issues that fester over time due to the fact that a couple is just uninformed or too embarrassed to ask. It is not uncommon for one spouse to experience various behaviors on the part of the other spouse and then find themselves totally confused – not knowing whether the behavior exhibited should be considered as something inappropriate or whether it is just the way marriage "is supposed to be". By reading and learning about how to *truly* become a "*We*" in a Torah marriage, many young and well-meaning *chasanim and kallahs* will now be equipped with **a point of reference** to know whether their marriage is progressing in the right direction or not.

In previous generations, much of what we cite in this handbook was a "*pashtus*" – it was taken for granted and was obvious. The proof to this is that in previous generations couples would generally remain married for their entire lives. Unfortunately, though, what was obvious one or two generations ago, is now very far from being obvious to the average chasan or kallah today.

As members of the "older generation" and after having had much more life and marriage experience than the young newlyweds we are marrying off, it is clear that it is now our **Torah obligation to *teach* our children as to how a Torah Marriage should look** – as part of the general *chinuch* (training) for life which we are obligated to supply them with[1].

---

1 See Kiddushin 30b, that a father is obligated **to teach** his son a profession based on the *pasuk* "*U're'ai chaim im ishah*" – "Just as a father has an obligation to *marry off* his son, so too he has an obligation *to teach him* a profession". Although the *pasuk* itself is essentially referring to the obligation that a father ensure that his son can engage successfully in a marriage, we can also learn out the obligation that a father ensure that his son can engage successfully in a profession. However, only when mentioning the obligation in regard to a profession, do Chazal use the wording that the father's obligation is *to teach* his son; in regard to marriage, Chazal did not use the wording that the father's obligation is *to teach* his son – only that he needs *to marry him off.* The reason for this difference is obvious: To *teach* one's son *how to be married,* was not something that was necessary for most all of history; the obligation of the father was *just* to "marry him off" and the son would know naturally "how to be married". We are all witnesses to our great grandparents and the chain of generations above them, who, for the vast majority, would live to a ripe old age and still remain married, even though no one had "*taught*" them how to do it. However, when we approach the times we live in today – which in many ways are *opposite* to the type of lifestyle that was lived in previous generations – it is becoming clearer and clearer that the rules of *how*

Although many years have passed since the original formulation of these rules, each time I review them I see how clearly it was the Yad Hashem that granted me the *zchus* to compile them in way that is easy to apply for the *to'eless* (benefit) of the Klal. As time goes on, there seems to be more and more of a need for couples who are starting, b'ezras Hashem, to build their *bayis ne'eman b'Yisrael,* to read a book of "directions" that can offer practical tools to guide them in their ever-ascending journey toward reaching true unity and mutual understanding.

It is my hope and *tefilah* that the tools presented here be helpful in guiding couples who are open and willing to do what they can to work on their relationship, to help them to know exactly *what it is* they have to work on in order to solidify their relationship in a lasting way. May these tools be helpful in strengthening and saving many young Jewish

---

to act in marriage and *how to remain* in a positive and lasting relationship are not just naturally known to the children. If so, it follows that nowadays it becomes an obligation upon every father *to teach* his son *how to be married* once he becomes of marriageable age, since this is implicitly included in the words of Chazal that "a father has an **obligation** *to marry off his son*": The obligation of a father was never *just* to marry off his son, but to do it in such a way that his son's marriage will *last*. Therefore, the obligation to *marry off* one's child certainly does not include any less of an obligation than the obligation to *teach* him a profession which is learned out from it; and if the times require that the child be taught *how to be married* in a way *that he can remain married* – then it becomes the parent's obligation to *teach him how* to do so.

marrieds from the waves of discord that are unfortunately so prevalent within the extended society today.

May Hashem help and bless his nation with Shalom, the utensil that holds all *brachah* (blessing)[2], and in the *zchus* of each of us working to establish Shalom in our homes, may we all merit to "*Hu ya'ase shalom aleinu*" – the One who makes Shalom Above, should make Shalom between all of us Yidden. May we then merit all the *brachos* of the *Geulah Shleima*, the Final Redemption, may it take place speedily in our days, *B'm'haira v'yamainu*, Amen.

Nachum Chaimowitz
Mar-Cheshvan 5780

---

2 *Uktzin* 3:12

Dedication

L'iluy Nishmas Mrs. Chaya Miriam Proctor a"h

Numerous years ago, when I had just decided to compile an initial draft of these rules, a tragedy occurred in our midst. The wife of one of my students, Mrs. Chaya Miriam Proctor *a"h*, was *niftar* at the age of forty after a prolonged illness. This was especially personal to me because her husband, *ybchl"ch*, Ahron Levi (Alan) Proctor, has been one of my closest students throughout all my years of teaching.

Mrs. Proctor's life was characterized by a strong desire to follow a life of Torah and mitzvos and connection to Hashem. After marrying Ahron Levi, she lived in a prominent community in Monsey where she was highly respected. She merited to have three children, Moshe Chaim, Avi and Chana Tova.

She excelled in the area of *tznius,* and she allowed her husband to dedicate many days and hours toward work for the Klal. Over the last 20 years, Ahron Levi has been actively involved in the proliferation of activities for "Chofetz Chaim Heritage Foundation" and "Partners in Torah". In addition, he has offered much free-of-charge successful business advice and practical tips to many other Kiruv organizations throughout the U.S. and Israel.

I saw it as *hashgachah* that this terrible loss had taken place just as I was about to write a concise guide to help young couples to reach the strongly desired and greatest goal of our lives: Shalom Bayis. It seemed to me to be only appropriate to dedicate the compilation of this sefer to her memory – *l'iluy nishmas* **Chaya Miriam bas Zev Halevi**: if she did not merit to continue to grow in *her* Shalom Bayis in this world, *may many others have the merit to do so,* and may this, in turn, be considered as a *zchus* and merit for her.

Acknowledgments

My personal thanks to the *chushuveh* (esteemed) Rabbonim *shlit"a* who took out from their precious time to review the manuscript: **Rabbi Yitzchak Berkovits, Rabbi Noach Orlowek,** and **Rabbi Binyomin Eisenberger. Rabbi Zecharya Greenwald** added suggested corrections which were incorporated into the sefer.

My father was unfortunately *niftar* before the printing of this sefer. May the publication of this sefer be an additional *zchus* for him, **Moshe Mendel ben Nachum** *a"h.*

May *ybchl"ch* my mother *tichye* merit to experience many more years of *nachas* from me and my family and may her unique support of Torah be a *zchus* for her both physically and spiritually.

It is clear that this sefer could not have been written without the ongoing, non-relenting support and care of my wife, Rebbetzin Ruchi Chaimowitz. May Hashem grant us continued years of health together in order to continue to actualize the directives of this sefer, and may we merit together to see Yiddishe *naches* from each one of our blessed children.

I thank **Hashem** for having given me the opportunity to counsel young married couples over the years and that the following guidelines have been helpful for them.

May Hashem help further and they prove helpful for all of the readers as well.

Introduction

"And the *Kruvim* … would face one another" (Shmos 25–20).

This was the optimum situation in the Mishkan (Gemara Yoma 54b); this is where Hashem's Holy Presence (the *Shechinah*) dwelt; and this is the level that every Jewish couple should aspire to reach.

But to be "facing one another" consistently is a hard level to reach. Every individual coming into marriage starts out as a "*Me*" and is facing in an *opposite* direction to his spouse. "Facing one another" with consistency will require taking the steps necessary **to transform the "Me" into a "We"**.

Many couples try to set this as a goal for themselves and work for countless years trying to achieve it, yet the rules of "how to do it practically" still evade them. How often we hear about people who listen to shiurim and read lengthy descriptions all about the *theory* of how to reach Shalom Bayis, only to come out thinking afterwards: "But how do I do this *practically?*"

The goal of "Marriage and Me" is to present the reader with easy-to-understand *practical steps* on how to reach this greatly sought after and desired goal.

The steps outlined in this handbook are divided into *three sections*. The first section gives the reader an understanding as to the *Purpose of Marriage* from a Torah perspective, and as to how the goal is supposed to look. The second section describes *The Natural Differences* that exist between every man and woman, so that the reader will be able to understand how to *Bridge the Gaps* when those differences inevitably arise in marriage. The third section discusses the *Key Tool* that is a necessity to use when bridging those gaps: *Healthy Communications.*

First, read all the steps and understand them (this is possible to do even before marriage). Then, once you are married and have some experience, go back and work on whatever step you need to improve on, little by little.

Slowly but surely – and, of course, **only with Siyata D'Shmaya** – we *do* have the ability to reach that greatest life-accomplishment of all: *Shalom Bayis.*

Chapter 1

Spiritual Goal

Your wedding day will undoubtedly be a happy occasion for everyone. But then comes the morning after, and you're faced with reality.

> Shalom Bayis starts even before getting married. Make sure that your goal in marriage together is a *spiritual* one rather than a *physical* one.

When the externalism of the wedding is receiving too much emphasis, this may be a sign that the focus of the couple themselves is too external.

> This can sometimes lead to feelings of externalism becoming adopted by the couple even after the wedding as a basis for communication, in place of a true relationship.

Such behavior tends to lead quite soon to misplaced priorities.

Therefore, even before getting married, make sure that your goal together is *spiritual*.

Example: Ideally you should discuss even before your *shidduch* is finalized, some specifics of what you hope to achieve together *spiritually*. It is common for couples to settle on statements such as: "Our goal in marriage is to become financially self-sufficient and to bring up our children in a religious, Jewish community". But this is still much too general.

A more specific example of a *spiritual* goal would be: "As we aim for all of the above, 1. We will **also** put effort into my husband[1] completing Shas or Mishnah Brura over the years; or 2. Into my husband becoming an active leader in a Mitzva or Kiruv project within the community; or 3. Into my husband taking his place as a leading donor to

---

1 The accomplishment of the husband is considered in *shomayim* as the spiritual accomplishment of his wife as well. This is because a woman offers the *counterbalance* necessary for her husband to accomplish his goals, without which he would not be able to achieve them (see Chapter 6). On a heavenly level this is considered as if she is just as much responsible for making the accomplishment possible as he (if not more, see footnote 37). This does not take away, however, from a woman's need to grow spiritually herself, **and it is clear that the spiritual plan of any couple needs to include an opportunity for the woman of the household to grow in her own spiritual understandings as well. This can continue onward throughout life by her attending shiurim, davenings, reading the sforim that speak to her, etc.**

support Mitzva causes, and to ardently keeping up a seder of *k'vias itim* (set daily times to learn or to attend a shiur)"[2].

---

2 Choosing one of the above examples really depends upon the inborn nature of the chasan, whether he be more gifted intellectually (first example), intuitively and emotionally (second example), or in his practical actualizing abilities (third example).

Once the couple has a unified, clear spiritual goal in mind, this will help to give all of their future life together a positive framework and perspective. True, just like every Jewish couple over the course of history, they will have to struggle with their unique challenges to try and maintain a life of Torah and *kiyum hamitzvos* and to raise their children to continue the holy Jewish chain; but at the same time, once they have set a *spiritual* goal, they will be able to measure their successes over time and to gain strength and *purpose* as they continuously grow closer toward what they had envisioned as their unique mission in life together. **Their Torah lifestyle will then not only be one long string of *mesirus nefesh* for the sake of passing down the *mesorah* to their children; it will also include the excitement and satisfaction they will share in their unified journey together toward reaching their spiritual ambitions.**

Chapter 2

Purpose of Marriage

The main goal of our lives can be achieved only once we become true "*givers*" and not remain "*takers*"[3].

Every human being is born naturally as a "*taker*"[4]. It

---

3 The purpose of creation was because Hashem Desires to Give Good to his creations (Sefer *Eitz Chaim, Sha'ar Hak'lalim, Perek Rishon*). Since the source of all good is found only within Hashem Himself, it is not possible for the creations to benefit from the true Good that Hashem wants to give them, unless they "become one" with Hashem (Derech Hashem, *Chelek Alef, Perek Beis, os alef*). The only way to "become one" with a spiritual entity is to be similar to him in characteristics (*Peirush Hasulam, P'sicha L'chochmas Hakabbalah, os yud-gimel*). **Since Hashem is the ultimate *Giver*, it is not possible to become similar to Him in all of His Characteristics, unless man also becomes a "*giver*".** For further explanation, see *It's All For The Good*, Part 1, Chapter 5.

4 "*Eiyar Pereh Adam yivaled*" – "[Like] a wild donkey is man born" (Iyov 11:12). See Chovos Halevavos (*P'sicha*) who explains that just as a wild donkey does not know of any restraints and just *takes* for himself because he does not recognize anyone giving to him, so too every man is born initially with no restraints in his focus on "*taking*" and satisfying his own personal needs.

is his job over the years to "turn around" his
"*taking*" nature and use it for the sake of "*giving*"[5].

The main opportunity in life to reach this
completion of ourselves is in marriage[6]. The purpose
of marriage is for both spouses to become true
"*givers*" to each other[7] and not to remain in a state of
always being a "*taker*" – the state that we were born
into.

Therefore, even before marriage, make sure that your
core motivation in getting married is for the purpose

---

5 According to the Kabbalah (See Eitz Chaim, *Chelek Beis, K. Abiyah, perek gimel,* and E"C 25:8), these are *preordained stages* in man's self-development. The first most visceral stage is expressed *from birth until adolescence,* and is a time where man's sole concern is *only* about "*taking*" to fill his own needs. The second stage takes place in the years of *adolescence,* when the sense of *giving* to another actually "gives" to him; however, at this stage it is still *mixed with the desire to* "*take*", and so the "*giving*" is not yet a complete *giving.* The third stage takes place approximately *at the age of 20* – marriageable age, and man now has the mature ability to choose and focus *all* of his energies toward *the pleasure* of *giving* to someone else, to the point that even when he "*takes*" – as a must in order to fill his own needs – it is also done with the intent of "*giving*" to another *through his taking.*

6 "*E'eseh Lo Eizer K'negdo*" – In essence each spouse *helps the other* by "giving" them *the opportunity to give* in the marriage - thus enabling them to become "like Hashem" (Ohev Yisrael, Parshas Eikev, piece beginning *V'y'ancha*).

7 A man fulfills this by fulfilling his obligations mentioned in the *kesubah* to provide food, clothing, etc. A woman fulfills this through allowing herself to *be taken care of* by her husband, as well as by "giving back" to him in the form of her support for his goals. See Chapters 5 and 12.

of "*giving*" to another **neshama** (soul), rather than for the purpose of "*taking*" for yourself[8].

When I ask students, "Why do you want to get married?" they offer a variety of reasons. Some say: "To have children". Others say: "To share life with someone and to have companionship". Yet others say: "It will help me with all the issues I've been dealing with since I was a child."

Then I go back and ask: From all of those reasons that you gave, how many of them are for the purpose of "*giving*", and how many of them are for the purpose of "*taking*"? Most students are very surprised to discover that all of the reasons they had to get married were just for the purpose of "*taking*".

Ideally your intent *even before marriage* should be in order to "*give*". To be **ready** for marriage means that you have already worked through your own personal issues to such an extent that you feel you are now

---

8 See Alei Shur (*Chelek Alef*, pgs. 249, 254) that the goal in marriage is that once you have worked on whatever *you* are lacking, you are now ready to take on another human being and to help *them* reach where *they* need to reach in life (this is also true in regard to each additional child who is born to the couple [Ibid]). **To get married with the intent of completing work that was needed to be done before marriage – or with the intent of "filling in" for a previous lack that was not dealt with yet – only results in more problems following marriage – not in solutions.**

ready to "take on another neshama and **to *give* them** what ***they*** need."

Once you are married, always check yourself to see whether your main intent in the relationship is in order "to give" or "to get".

In order for the marriage to function optimally, your main focus should be upon *giving* to your spouse even more than it is on *taking* for yourself[9] [see footnote]. Most all of the issues that surface in marriage are a result of one or both spouses concentrating only upon "*taking*" for themselves, without showing ***any true concern*** for the needs of the other.

In a non-Torah based marriage, it is very common that each partner in the relationship is coming from a

---

9 **Disclaimer:** This does not mean that you should ever have to ignore your most basic needs because you would like *only* to give to your spouse. **It is understood, a priori, that in order to give to another there must first be a "you".** *"V'ahavta l'raiachah"* is only possible if first there is a *"kamocha"*, and you have addressed all of *your own* basic needs. To ignore yourself and still push to give to another, will only result eventually in not having any strength left to give anymore, and then both of you, you and the receiver of your giving, will have lost out. What is being stated here is that once you *have already* given to yourself, and you *already have* all of your own most basic needs taken care of, **then**, when you turn your attention toward such accomplishments which go *beyond your most basic needs* in life, your focus should be more upon *giving* to your spouse rather than on acquiring more for yourself.

perspective of "**take**". "What do you have to *give me?*" is the thought in the back of each spouse's mind even if they don't verbalize it.

This causes both partners to start off their marriage with the goal of *getting* as much as they can from the other. The problem is that once there is nothing left to "*get*" anymore, they have no reason to remain married.

In a Torah marriage, however, the way it's supposed to be is that each partner is coming from a position of "**give**". "What do I have to *give to you* – to help *you* become everything that *you* can become?" is the thought that should be in the back of every chasan and kallah's mind, even if they don't verbalize it[10].

This will cause both the chasan and the kallah to start off their marriage with the focus of how much they

---

10 One should not object at this point by saying: "But if I don't worry for myself, then who will worry for *me?*" In contrast to the secular mind-set of marriage where each spouse subconsciously thinks: "I'm number one; and you're number two", the Jewish mind-set of marriage is where each spouse subconsciously thinks: "I'm number two; and *you're* number one". When the marriage is working properly, a person who focuses on what his spouse needs, need not be concerned about what will happen with his needs. In the same way that he is focused on fulfilling his spouse's needs, so too will his spouse be focused on filling *his* needs. This setup makes for the strongest bond in marriage, because each spouse is focused upon taking care of *the other's* needs even more than they are focused upon taking care of their own, and so both spouses' needs end up getting met in the most bonding way possible.

can *give* to each other rather than on how much they can "*get*".

When the focus is on *giving* rather than on *getting*, the excitement of your marriage and intensity of your relationship will not only be for the short-term but can remain alive for the entire length of your lives together.

Chapter 3

What is "Shalom"?

Building a **"Bayis"** where there is **"Shalom"** is the greatest achievement that you can aspire to in your Torah life. Why?

> Everything we're trying to accomplish on a *worldly* level is the proliferation of Hashem's Name in a positive way throughout the entire world[11]. The "worst" **aveira** (transgression) possible is to intentionally erase Hashem's Name, because it is

---

11 **Devorim 26:17**: "*Es Hashem he'emartah hayom l'hiyos lecha l'Elokim*" – *you have made known* to the world today that Hashem is your G-d (Ramban). **Berachos 6a:** *You made me known* as One (*chativa achas*) in the world". See also Rashi to **Bereishis 24:7** that Avraham Avinu said: "Now He is G-d of the heaven and G-d of the earth because I have familiarized the beings to talk about Him; but [originally] when He took me from my father's house, He was [only known as] G-d of the heavens and not G-d of the earth – that the people of the world did not *know* about Him." Our fulfilling of Torah u'mitzvos leads to our national goal in *this* world, of making the Greatness of Hashem *known* to everyone in the world.

diametrically opposite to *everything* we're trying to do in a life of Torah.

Yet Hashem is willing to allow that His Holy Name, which was written just like it is in a sefer Torah, to be erased twice – intentionally – for the purpose of bringing about Shalom in one "Bayis" – between **one** man and his wife[12]. How could this be?

> The revelation of Hashem's Holy Name which takes place when a couple lives with true Shalom among themselves, is **much, much greater** than the revelation which takes place by writing Hashem's Name on a parchment. Our goal of revealing Hashem's Holy Name in a positive way throughout the entire world will be much better accomplished through the achievement of Shalom Bayis – **even amongst one couple** – than through the written Name of Hashem on a Torah parchment.

I once asked a student, "What is the worst *aveira* (transgression) you can think of? No, I don't mean which one receives the worst punishment, nor do I mean the one which a person is obligated to give up his life for. What I mean is the one which is most

---

12 Bamidbar 5:23; Gemara Sukkah 53b.

opposite to everything we're trying to accomplish in *this* world through fulfilling the Torah and mitzvos."

It took him a while, and eventually I gave him my answer. "The worst conceivable sin – in my understanding – is to willingly blot out Hashem's Name; because everything we're trying to do through Torah and mitzvos is to proliferate Hashem's Name in the world in a positive way[13] (*kiddush Hashem*). If there were any way we could beautifully plaster His Name over all of creation, or if we could hang gigantic banners carrying His Name over every significant spot in the world which would impart a real message to all the nations of the world as to how great Hashem really is, we would do it[14].

"When a *sofer* writes Hashem's Name in a Sefer Torah after having the proper intent and preparation, the parchment then becomes so sanctified that we consider it just like a "living" Jewish soul – to the point where if it were destroyed

---

13 See footnote 11.

14 In a sense, in regard to ourselves this is really what we do when we "picture" Hashem's Name opposite our eyes in everything we do (see Mishna Brura, Siman Alef, *seif-katan* daled, in the name of the Ari *z"l*). We are in effect "posting" His Name before our eyes in everything we do.

(*chas v'shalom*), we would perform a *levayah* for it[15].

> "So to intentionally scratch out Hashem's Name, from upon a Torah parchment is the worst conceivable *aveira*".

Yet Hashem is willing to allow that His Holy Name, written on parchment in holiness, be erased – twice – just in order to bring about Shalom between *one* man and his wife[16].

---

15 *Sheilos U'tshuvos* Divrei Chaim, 2, *likutim* 1.

16 The Gemara in Makos (11a) tells us that when Dovid Hamelech was digging the foundations for the Bais Hamikdash, the digging ran so deep that it struck the "*t'hom*" – the layer of sub-terrestrial waters that lies deep beneath the ground. The amount and force of water that began to rise toward ground level posed a danger of massive flooding and was life-threatening. Dovid Hamelech decided that the urgency of the situation called for using Hashem's Holy Name to perform a miracle and stop the waters from rising. He wanted to write Hashem's Name on a piece of clay and throw it into the rising waters, in order that the Holy Name should miraculously reinstate the waters in their proper place beneath the ground. There was only one problem: Even if the miracle would work, the Name of Hashem would become erased by the water. Maybe to do so intentionally was such a severe sin that it would be prohibited even in the face of a *pikuach nefesh* (life-threatening) situation. He quickly called out: "Does anyone know the answer to this *shaila* (halachic question)? Say the answer right now!"

Among the crowd, there was a wise man from the Sanhedrin named Achitofel, who knew the answer. He said: "We see that **in order to bring about Shalom between a man and his wife, the Torah allows that the Name of Hashem that was written with holiness, be erased twice.** In this case, where the Shalom of the entire world is at stake, most certainly Hashem would allow His Name to be erased." And so Dovid Hamelech took the piece of pottery with Hashem's Name on it, threw it into the rising waters, and they subsided, returning to their

The only way to understand this logically is to conclude that what is accomplished by building one "Bayis" where Shalom reigns – even if it be only among *one* couple in Klal Yisrael – is *greater* than the proliferation of Hashem's Name to the eyes of the entire world.

This is because, on the parchment the Holy Name of Hashem stands "*still*"; in a Jewish home it is *alive*.

When a couple merits and they can live together in peace and harmony, **they themselves** create the revelation of Hashem's Holy Name. The unity of the Holy Letter *Yud* that is included in the man's name, and the Holy Letter *Heh* that is included in the woman's name, create a *living* revelation of Hashem's Name in the world[17].

It is worth "giving up" the "smaller" revelation for the greater one.

We see clearly from this, that to maintain a "Bayis" where there exists true unity between a couple *is the*

---

original sub-terrestrial level. This source shows us clearly the supreme value of Shalom Bayis in a Torah lifestyle.

17 Gemara Sotah (17a): "*Darash* Rabbi Akiva, *Ish V'Isha: zachu – Shechina bainaihen*". Rashi explains: "Behold, Hashem has divided His Name and settled it between them – *Yud* in [the word] *Ish*, and *Heh* in [the word] *Ishah*."

greatest and most valuable achievement that we can accomplish in our Torah lives.

Chapter 4

The Greatest Goal: Building a "Bayis"

"Darchei (The Ways of) **Shalom**" in the words of
Chazal, applies specifically to a situation where there
is a *clear contrast of two opposite natures.*

> Chazal say: "*We* strengthen the hands of *Non-Jews* in
> the year of Shviis … and *we* inquire in *their* well-being
> and greet them – because of "*Darchei Shalom*"[18].

This teaches us in regard to the use of the word
"**Shalom**" wherever it appears:
"Shalom" *is not* when there are *no* differences;
"Shalom" *is* when there *are* differences and you can
bridge over them successfully[19].

---

18 Mishna in Gittin (61a).
19 Sefer Alei Shur, *Chelek Alef,* p.258.

This greatly alters our whole perception of "**Shalom Bayis**". If a couple is married for 6 months, and *no differences at all* have surfaced between them, it is not yet considered that they have achieved "**Shalom Bayis**"; it only tends to indicate that such a couple has hardly reached the level of closeness and understanding where they are conversing truly and openly[20].

> The concept of a couple getting married and walking away "happily ever after", exists only in Hollywood; in real life, however, **it is not possible** that a couple should spend 24/7 together, and that there not be some opposing *differences* that surface between them in their characters and technical approach[21].

Only once differences between the couple *have* arisen and it is apparent they have *opposite* natures, and *then*, they are able to successfully **bridge over** those differences, is it considered that they have achieved "**Shalom**" in their Bayis.

> Although we believe that on the spiritual level the two *neshamos* (souls) are really one[22], that does not

---

20 Ibid.

21 Ibid, p. 257.

22 Sefer HaZohar, Vayikra, 81b.

contradict the fact that when the *neshamos* descend physically into this world they spend their childhood years as *two separate people*. During those years they become conditioned to different approaches of how to balance their specific, individual needs. This necessitates that once the two are reunited again when they get married, that not only they unite physically in the building of their home, but that they also unite interactively in their different natures and conditioned lifestyles as well. This will necessitate that they "bridge over" the differences between them when they inevitably arise.

Shalom in your Bayis does not take place just by you deciding to totally *nullify* yourself to your spouse; rather, it takes place by constantly **building bridges** that will facilitate unity while you both *remain* the unique different individuals that you are.

If so, in order for you to be able to *"**bridge over the differences**"* when they arise, it is necessary to be aware of certain natural differences that exist between *every* man and woman in the world.

Chapter 5

Difference One:
The Emotional Level –
Strength vs. Softness

In order that a man and a woman come to truly complement and complete one another, Hashem has woven two opposite facets into their emotional makeup.

> Man was designed in a deep emotional way, as the partner who feels satisfaction from filling the role of *giving care* in a relationship; and a woman as the partner who feels satisfaction from *being taken care of*[23].

---

23 The mitzvah of Kiddushin is described in the Torah as *"Ki yikach ish isha"* – "When **a man shall acquire** a woman" (Devorim 24:1), and the Gemara in Kiddushin (5b) states explicitly that this means that the man must be the initiator and the *"giver"* in the Kiddushin process. "[If] *he* gave [the money] (which is similar to *"Ki yikach"*-Rashi) … it is Kiddushin; … [If] *she* gave [the money] … it is not Kiddushin." The Torah is very clear by means of this *halachic* requirement, that it specifically be *the man* who is the

This is the *first* difference we need to bridge over. Since a man was created to fill the role of *giving care,* his uniqueness is most apparent when he exhibits the qualities of "Strength" and "Caring" for his wife[24]. Since a woman was created to fill the role of one who is *taken care of,* her uniqueness is most apparent when she shows the qualities of "Softness" and "Acceptance" toward her husband [25].

> To bridge this gap a woman needs to accept and allow the man to be the leading figure in regard to caring for the *spiritual* and *financial* direction of their home. By her allowing herself *to be cared for* as a result of his lead, she is actually filling a need of his[26]. When

one to initiate the marriage process. This Torah guideline holds within it the sublime message that the Torah's view regarding the marital bond is that it specifically be *the man* who initiates - and, as such, that he be the one who takes responsibility to fill in whatever is needed for the basic functionality and continuation of the marriage. This idea is further underscored by the Torah prohibition for a man to ever deny his wife any of her basic needs such as food and clothing (*Lo Ta'aseh* 262). We do not find that a woman has any such Torah responsibility toward her husband. Although both husband and wife are *givers* to each other and *receivers* from each other in the marriage relationship, it is specifically *the man* from whom the Torah expects to *give care.* In contrast, the woman's part in completing the initial Kiddushin, is just the fact that she now entrusts herself and *allows herself to be cared for* by her husband. See footnote 93.

24 See footnote 69.

25 Avodas Yisrael, Pesach, piece beginning *Yavo Dodi.*

26 See footnote 85 that a man has an actual *need* to feel that his wife is happy with his leadership of the family.

he leads the house in a "Confident" – yet "Caring" – way, her allowing herself *to be cared for* will then bring her to feel a natural sense of respect for the leadership role that he plays.

Being gifted with the qualities of "Strength" and "Caring", *it is the man* who needs to infuse his home with a *spiritual* feel which will breed a positive desire for connection to Hashem.

The story is told of a young married man who came to the third Belzer Rebbe, Rabbi Yissaschar Dov Rokeach *zy"a*, presenting his dire plea that the Rebbe help him save his Shalom Bayis. The Rebbe asked him whether he was accustomed to recite *birkas HaTorah* in the morning in his home out loud[27]. When the young man answered that he did not, the Rebbe advised him that he should begin to do so. After a few months, the young man came back to the Rebbe with the good news that his Shalom Bayis had greatly improved.

The young man stood before the Rebbe with

---

27 Obviously, this does not mean that a man should *yell* the brachos in the morning – especially if his wife is still sleeping. What it means is that within the home there needs to be some relatable expression of his real feelings for Hashem and the Torah.

astonishment, begging for some explanation of how this had worked. The explanation that he received was as follows:

A woman is constantly looking for reasons to respect her husband. The primary way that she gains respect for him, is when *she can experience* a greater level of spiritual connection *for herself through him*. Even if her husband is very connected spiritually, but his connection is expressed only when he is in the *Beis Midrash* and not when he is at home, there will be something lacking in *her experience of his spirituality.* By saying the *birkas HaTorah* out loud in his home with enthusiasm and concentration, the husband allows for his wife to find *a point of her own spiritual connection* through the expression of his spirituality, and thus she can come to respect him more.

> This is just one example of how a husband sets the *spiritual* "tone" for his home. The tone of spirituality that a man infuses within the home is imperative for the healthy spiritual growth of the husband and wife as a couple.

Also included as part of exhibiting a strong example as the "spiritual provider" for his home, a man needs to have some knowledge of basic Halachos, such as

Hilchos Shabbos, Kashrus, and other Halachos that are applicable in the home[28].

It is important to note in this context, that although every young married man aspires to develop spiritually and to express *strength* in his learning experience, he should be careful not relate to his wife as his *chavrusa*[29]. She relates to his spirituality from *her* perspective[30].

The man is also the one who needs to be the leading figure in regard to the *financial* direction of the home, and to come up with a viable plan of how to support the family[31]. The more assertive a man is to set a

---

28 Ideally, a man should dedicate some time before his marriage to study at least peripherally those areas of halacha that are applicable within the home. This does not mean that he needs to become a Rav, but it does mean that he should at least be aware of what may be a *shailah* – a Halachic question – in those areas that are most prone for questions to arise in the home.

29 This does not mean that a couple cannot organize a daily or weekly learning time together. It simply means that a man should not expect that his experience in learning with his wife will be the same sort of experience that he has when learning with his chavrusa in the *Beis Midrash*.

30 If a man shares with his wife a Torah insight that to him may be very simple and brief, but she sees in his eyes the *excitement* he has about this new insight, this itself may often be enough for her to feel spiritual growth from the Torah – although it does not include the complicated depth that the man is used to in his learning.

31 The fact that according to Torah this obligation rests on the *man,* is clear from the wording that Chazal have established in the *Kesuvah*: "And I will work, and honor and feed and support you".

pleasant, caring, and *spiritual* tone in the home *and* to actualize a viable plan of *financial* support, the more accepting a woman will be and allow herself *to be cared for* through her husband's lead and to be supportive in helping him to implement his viable plans[32]. Creating this *bridge* on the *emotional* level, is certainly an enormous step forward toward helping the couple to access the quality of Shalom they so yearn for and to have it dwell in a consistent way in their Bayis.

Thus a man is responsible to come up with some sort of viable financial plan for his family. Even if the plan never materializes, it is still necessary within the context of *hishtadlus,* to develop some plan that *could* work. (**Note:** Even if the plan is that at the present time it is the wife who will be the main breadwinner for the house, **it is the man who needs to be the one to formulate and to *take responsibility* for such a plan.**) To live without any financial plan – according to in the Mishna in Pirkei Avos (2:2) – will soon bring to *bitul* Torah and possibly even transgression, *ch"v.* Unfortunately, because making an honest living today has become so difficult and pressured, many men today radiate a sense of weakness when it comes to fulfilling their financial obligations to their family. In order to maintain the true position of the man, it is necessary nowadays that a man find the strength in himself to invest into doing both the *hishtadlus* necessary to earn an honest living *as well as* to project his heartfelt *bitachon* in Hashem, that once he has already done all that is truly required of him from the *hishtadlus* perspective, he will undoubtedly have whatever his family needs, to live with a sense of *Yishuv hada'as* (peace of mind).

32 See also footnote 87.

Chapter 6

Difference Two: The Thinking Level – Abstract vs. Practical

Being that men and women play different roles in complementing each other and in building their household, Hashem has also imbued them with different *thought patterns* to accomplish their respective goals.

> Since a man's role is to provide both spiritually and financially for his home, a man's nature is **to think more about world-wide, *less practical ideas*.**

Because a woman's role is to accept her husband's "lead" on the spiritual and financial levels, and that position requires her to concentrate on how to use the finances and "raw materials" that the man gathers

from the outside world *in a practical way*, her nature is
**to think more about the"hands-on" practical side
of things.**

> When Hashem originally created man, the intent
> was to allow a *spiritual* soul to come to this *physical*
> world in order that he be tested with a choice between
> physicality (*taking* only for himself) and spirituality
> (*giving* to his Source, Hashem). By means of his
> choosing spirituality over physicality from his *own*
> initiative, man would then merit to all the good of the
> world-to-come[33] because he would become a *giver* –
> like Hashem[34]. In order to be placed in such a situation
> that would require him to make a real choice[35], man
> would have to actively be involved in procuring all
> of his physical ["*taking*"] needs: to eat, drink, have
> shelter etc., *while at the same time* be actively involved
> in pursuing his spiritual ["*giving*"] goal: building

33 Because it had come from his own initiative, man could then receive in the
form of reward all the good that Hashem wanted to give him, and would not be
embarrassed to receive it – see Da'as Tvunos from the Ramchal, *ois yud-tes*.

34 See *It's All For The Good*, Part 1, Chapter 6.

35 This is a description of man's test *after* the *chait* (sin) of Adam Harishon. Prior
to that all of man's physical needs were taken care of by the *malachim* (Sanhedrin
59b), and his test was focused only on the choice between the physical "taking"
considerations – represented by the *Eitz Hada'as* and the spiritual consideration
of "*giving*" to Hashem by listening to His forbidding ordinance – no matter what.

a *giving* relationship with Hashem by gaining an understanding of Hashem, Torah, and of the heavenly realities above in order *to connect to Him.* All of this was initially needed to be done by one person.

What Hashem did in the *ma'amar* (proclamation) of "*Lo tov heyos ha'odom l'vado*"[36] – "It is not good that man be alone", was that He divided that being into two: now every *neshama* that would come into the world would be divided into two halves. One half would be primarily involved in the procuring of the *physical* needs for both, while the other half would be primarily involved in grasping the deeper *spiritual* realities – the achievement of which would merit equal spiritual reward and connection to Hashem for *both.* Even the half of the *neshama* that would constantly toil to arrange all the *physical* needs to allow for the other half to connect to Hashem through its understanding of His Torah, would receive *the same exact amount of reward* as the half that had learned Torah – since it would only be *because of that preparation and support* that such a level of connection to Hashem was reached[37].

____

36 Breishis 2:18.

37 According to the Midrash, in a certain way the supporter of Torah has *an even greater importance* than the person who learns Torah himself; see Breishis Rabbah

> A man is the part of the *neshama* that was created
> to go *beyond* the practical realm and to seek
> understanding of the *spiritual* realms above;
> therefore his natural thought process is generally to
> be more **abstract**, something that will help him to
> reach his goal of grasping the levels *beyond*[38].

99:8 where it is emphasized that Zevulun, who supported the Torah learning of Yissachar, is actually mentioned by the Torah *prior* to Yissachar.

38 I once heard from one of my *Chushuveh* and esteemed Rabbeim *z"l* (My Rebbe in *hashkafah*, Rav Chaim Yaakov Goldvicht *z"l* (1935–1995), The Ba'al *Asufas Ma'arochos*, who was a close talmid of the *Chazon Ish* and a scion of the Belzer family lineage), an amazing explanation on the Gemara in Yevamos (63a). The Gemara cites a conversation that Rabbi Yosi had on occasion when he merited to meet Eliyahu HaNavi: "The Pasuk says, 'And I shall make for him a *helpmate* (Breishis 2:18)'. In what way does a woman help a man?" Eliyahu HaNavi answered: "A man brings home wheat kernels from the field – does he eat the wheat? A man brings home flax – does he wear the flax? Doesn't it become clear that she is the one who brings light to his eyes and stands him on his feet?". Rav Goldvicht asked, "Everything that this Gemara says seems so obvious from a *physical* perspective. Why was it necessary that the Holy Tanah Rabbi Yosi ask for this explanation from Eliyahu HaNavi?" He answered that Rabbi Yosi knew that whenever Hashem uttered a *"Ma'amar"* in the creation of the world (the pasuk of *"E'eseh Lo Eizer"* begins with the word *"V'yomer"*, and is enumerated in Sforim Hakedoshim as being the tenth *Ma'amar* that the world was created with [as mentioned in Pirkei Avos 5 – 1]), its importance was for the purpose of completing a part of creation that was still needed in order to bring the world to its completion on the **spiritual** level. And so his question was: "How does a woman help a man to attain the **spiritual** level of connection to Hashem that he is expected to reach?" It was specifically in regard to *this* point, how a woman helps a man on the **spiritual** level, that Eliyahu HaNavi revealed these principles. See explanation in the continuation of this chapter.

A woman was created as that part of the *neshama* that focuses on the *physical* needs of man, and she consistently invests time, energy and thought into how best to prepare all of the *physical* necessities. Therefore a woman's natural thought process is generally to be more **practical**, something that will help her to reach her goal of filling man's physical needs and supporting him to grow in his grasp of the levels beyond, thus connecting more to Hashem.

> This insight affords us an amazing understanding as to the differences that naturally exist between the natures of every man and woman. To summarize, the general rule is, that among any given couple the thought pattern of the man will always tend to be that much more *theoretical and abstract,* and of the woman that much more *practical and "hands-on"*[39].

---

39 This does not mean to say that there cannot be men who are very practically oriented, and women who are very theoretically oriented. Quite to the contrary, it is very often that there are couples where the man is the much more practically oriented partner and the woman is the more out-of-the-house and "theoretical – worldly oriented" partner. It just means, that if we were to organize *all* the men in the world into a list according to their level of being practical vs. being theoretical – where each man would be placed in the position on the list where he would be below the man in the world who is more theoretical than him and above the man in the world who is more practical than him – and then we would do the same in a list for *all* the women in the world, we would find that for any given **parallel point** on both lists, the man will have more of a natural tendency toward being theoretical, and the woman

Because of man's intrinsic nature which lends itself toward being more *theoretical and abstract,* he is naturally prone to concentrate on things that are *beyond* his immediate reality. Therefore, even when it comes to filling his most technical needs he focuses specifically on the part that needs to be accessed from the "larger world beyond": acquiring the raw materials, earning the funds, etc. He brings all the produce and raw products home from the field, but it is not his intrinsic nature to then invest the time, energy and thought into the practical preparation of his food or clothing. If it were up to him, a man would just chew the wheat kernels that he brought home, and would probably piece together some flimsy covering for himself rather than soak the flax, comb it into strands, weave it, dye it and then sew it into a garment with the right measurements[40].

> If man were to do that, he would end up not feeling very happy or satisfied from his meals or clothing. He might get by on the kernels, but then

more of a natural tendency toward being practical. But certainly it is possible to find many men who are more practically oriented than many women, and many women who are more theoretical than many men. See also footnote 43.

40 Yevamos 63a. See footnote 38.

there would never be any twinkle in his eye or any enthusiasm for his life. Eventually he would weaken both emotionally and physically from such a lifestyle, and would not even be able to stand on his own two feet[41]. This would hardly allow him to continue to invest energy in his primary goal, which is to gain a knowledge of Hashem.

A woman, through her unique nature of being more *practical,* in effect "lights up his eyes and stands him on his feet"[42], so that man can continue to grow consistently throughout his life in his connection to Hashem. Isn't this the best possible helpmate that man could ever hope for in order to obtain his *spiritual* goals?

> The knowledge of this natural difference in the *thinking processes* of men and women can already help us greatly to bridge many of the gaps when the differences arise[43].

---

41 Ibid.

42 Wording of the Gemara in Yevamos (63a).

43 When learning this it is essential to remember, that all the rules are simply *generalizations* whose purpose is to help as *tools* to form bridges and for each couple to attain their **own** Shalom Bayis respectively. If a certain generalization is *not* helpful and *not* applicable in a given couple's situation, then it is clear that the goal of such a couple is for them to find their **own** individual and unique balance

In order to bridge over this gap, both spouses must *understand from the onset* that the natural thought patterns they each have when viewing any issue, will be *opposite perspectives to each other.*

---

according to who *they are* – rather than to try and alter their natures in order to fit the generalization. For example, if there is a couple where the woman is clearly the one who is more *theoretical* and the one who can deal better with the needs that extend beyond the realm of the house, and the man is clearly the one who is more *practical* and the one who can deal better with the "hands-on" needs within the house, then that couple should clearly build the bridges between themselves that are applicable for **their particular reality according to who they are.** This does not mean though, that in such an instance the generalizations themselves have no value to the couple as tools; even a couple whose reality is the *opposite* of the generalization, can still gain benefit and extrapolate insights and advice from the understanding of the generalization, as to how they themselves can best achieve their own unique balance according to their situation.

Chapter 7

Learning to Appreciate an Opposite Perspective

Every viewpoint has its aspect of truth. When you can share with others the truth of *your* viewpoint, and you can listen to the aspect of truth in *their* viewpoint, you can then bridge between both of your opinions and reach the right answer for each individual situation. Therefore, it is of the *essence,* that you be able *to appreciate the aspect of truth* in a perspective which is opposite to yours.

> The Torah teaches us: "It is not good for man to be alone". A woman's natural ability to perceive any situation **practically** – is the counterbalance that helps a man keep his feet "**on the ground**".

On the one hand, a woman is gifted with thinking

more about practical, 'hands-on" ideas; but because of this she is prone to overlook the importance of an idealistic viewpoint. Therefore a woman must balance her viewpoint by training herself to value a more *abstract* viewpoint – even though, naturally, she might see it as not having any connection to "real" life – in order to reach the greatest level in her worship of Hashem that she can reach[44].

On the other hand, a man's gift is to think more about world-wide less practical ideas; but because of this, he is prone to overlook the practical side of any given

---

44 This is a reason why it is hard for a woman to show acceptance when her husband expresses his "dreams". The reason that a man tends to have "big dreams" is because his innate nature, which corresponds to his specific *tikun* (correction) in this world, is to think about more world-wide, less practical ideas. Very often, men who exhibit their natural tendency to be "dreamers", are perceived by their spouses as being "unrealistic" or that "they don't get it". The practical side of a woman allows her to immediately see the fallacy in a plan which is above the family's means or outside of the realm of actualization. The value, however, in a man's natural tendency to think beyond the practical realm, is that his tangible connection to a lofty goal, can actually give direction over time to all the effort which the family is investing in just to survive, to position it within the framework of a greater purpose and life goal. Therefore, it is also very important from a perspective of "balance", that a woman not nullify or "knock down" her husband's "dreams" in a condescending manner. Although she knows in her heart that practically it is of primary concern that the family survive and so she will not allow anything to take place which is a risk or threatening to the family's stability, nonetheless she should also show respect and validity for her husband's ability to "frame" the direction of their lifestyle toward a larger, long-term goal, by listening to his propositions in an active, participative and understanding way.

situation. Therefore a man must balance his viewpoint by training himself to focus more on the *practical* side of each situation – in order to reach the greatest level in his worship of Hashem that he can reach.

Some areas that a man can work on recognizing the "practical side" of a situation, are:

1. He should be careful not to overlook *his own physical needs.*

2. He should be careful not to overlook *his wife's physical needs.*

3. He should be careful not to overlook his *wife's accomplishments.*

4. He should be careful not to overlook *communications.*

5. Ultimately, he should be careful not to overlook *the basic needs of the home.*

> Being positioned as leader of his household, forces a man to consider the **practical** needs of each situation, something which is hard for him to do by nature, since his tendency is to concentrate on ideas that are **beyond** the practical realm. However, this should not be considered as a step "*downward*" for a man; **on the contrary,** it is a huge step **upwards** toward attaining the completeness and greatness that he is so trying to reach.

1. He should be careful not to overlook his own physical needs.

> **Example:** A man should realize that when he is caught up in the throes of some "world level" accomplishment (i.e. preparing a shiur for many people, sealing a large business deal, organizing the shul's yearly benefit, etc.) his natural tendency is not to eat enough, not to sleep enough, etc. He must therefore take into consideration when finding himself in such circumstances, to *maintain the balance* of his physical needs by filling all of them appropriately.

2. He should be careful not to overlook his wife's physical needs.

> **Example:** A man should be aware that his wife's physical endurance is probably not the same as his own. If a couple needs to walk two blocks away to get a taxi – but they are traveling with three heavy suitcases – a man should realize that his wife's physical abilities are not the same as his own, and he should not automatically expect her to carry even one of the suitcases, and to follow his pace.

This point runs even deeper. Since a woman was created as being naturally *"softer"* than a man, it follows that she has a very real emotional need, as different than that of a man's, to feel *cared for*. When a man uses his natural ability at being "*stronger*" than a woman to show that he *takes care* of his wife, he thus fills a very real need that she has. This only adds to strengthen the bond among them as a couple. Most certainly a man *should never use* his quality of being naturally "*stronger*" to ignore or to *not show any care* for his wife's needs, because that itself would serve to weaken their bond as a couple.

3. He should be careful not to overlook his wife's accomplishments.

> **Example:** A man should realize that by nature when he is caught up in the throes of some "world level" accomplishment he is naturally prone not to realize or appreciate his wife's achievements at home. Especially during such times, he should practice when coming home, that his first inquiries be *about his wife's accomplishments*. He needs to shift his focus from the "world-level" to the practical level before he walks into the door[45]. He needs to remind himself that in Hashem's book, his wife's cooking of the food,

---

45 This practice is mentioned here in regard to a man's natural *thinking* pattern. See also Chapter 11 – number 1, for an additional important reason that a man train himself with this practice.

bathing the children, and cleaning the house, *have no less importance* than his sealing a multi-million dollar business deal, or of his raising enough funds to marry off a needy Chasan and Kallah.

4. He should be careful not to overlook communications.

Example: A man needs to be aware that when he is outside and is caught up in some "world level" pursuit, he is naturally prone *to forget* about calling home. Once he is married, he needs to understand the value of having a "home base", namely, someone who is at home waiting for him [46]. Specifically at such times, when he is caught up in a "world-level project", he should remind himself to take out the time to call home, to communicate where he is, and to notify his wife how much longer it seems it will take before he comes home.

5. Ultimately, he should be careful not to overlook the basic needs of the home.

Example: A common dialogue among couples often sounds like this:

Wife: "One minute, take out the garbage!" (calling out

---

46 See footnote 72.

after her husband as he sprints out of the door in the morning).

Husband: "Can't you see how late I am? The bus is leaving in one minute; I'll take it out when I come home!"

A man needs to understand why this cliché answer is unacceptable.

> He is assuming that what takes place in his Kollel or workplace is *infinitely greater* than the insignificant act of taking out the garbage. Since his tendency is to relate naturally more to his spiritual or world-level accomplishments, it seems to him that what can be accomplished by applying himself toward his pursuits during the extra minutes he is in Kollel or involved in a business deal at work, will help him to reach much greater heights in his *avodas* Hashem than by exerting himself physically to remove the garbage bag from the kitchen.

In reality though, it is exactly this act of *taking care* of his home that makes him all the greater in his *avodas* Hashem. By taking responsibility for the *practical* needs of his home, a man strikes a balance between his lofty and more removed nature, and his wife's practical and "down-to-earth" nature – thus reaching *true* greatness.

> "Rabbi Yochanan said: Wherever you find [mentioned in the verse] the Awesomeness of Hashem, you find [cited next to it] the Humility of Hashem[47]".

The simple meaning of this statement is that Hashem acts humbly, and even after mention of His Greatness, He immediately makes sure to mention the "small acts" He does as well[48].

> However, this teaching can also be understood to mean, that the revelation of *real Awesomeness and Greatness* is only attained *according to the amount of Humility* – of being able to humble one's self to those who are *below* him and to those who are dependent upon him.

Real greatness is defined by *how much a person can humble himself to those who are smaller than him*, and how much he exhibits that through his actions.

> Therefore, if you are faced with the choice of taking

---

47 Megillah 31b.

48 See Rambam Sefer Hamitzvos, Mitzvas Aseh 8, that the Positive Mitzva in the Torah of "*V'halachta b'drachav*", is that we pattern our middos after those that we find in the Torah are the descriptions of the Holy Attributes of Hakadosh Baruch Hu. Therefore the simple meaning of the Gemara Megillah is that we should train ourselves to act with humility, just as we find that Hashem acts with humility.

out the garbage and *showing care for your wife* or ignoring her requests so that you can gain some precious extra moments of Kollel or work time, it is clear that what will bring you *closest* to Hashem is when you can use your *strength* and ability to appreciate the *practical* side of things, and when you can *show care* through your actions for that specific person who counterbalances you and *who is dependent upon you.*

Chapter 8

Make Sure You Have a Family Rav

In order to properly bridge the gaps when the differences arise, it necessary that every couple – already from the first weeks of their marriage – decide upon one halachically-accepted Rav whom they feel comfortable with, whom they both accept upon themselves to be their *family* Rav.

> Now that we have seen how men and women are "pre-programmed" to have different thinking patterns, it is quite clear that in order for a marriage to work and for the two individuals to interact as one, it will require a lot of "looking beyond self" and a desire to truly understand the other and care for **their** needs in order to "bridge the gaps".

However, sometimes, even when one's focus is on *giving* and understanding the differences, he is still not able to consent to what his spouse's understanding is because it seems to him to be against **what Hashem wants**.

> Similar to what takes place in **halachah** (Jewish Torah Law) when there is a **machlokes** (difference of opinion) between two *talmidei chachamim* (Sages) – that they cannot compromise on their views because each believes that only *his* view is truly the Ratzon Hashem[49] (Will of G-d) – so too can often take place in the difference of opinion between a couple. As much as they would like to be *giving* to one another, they may feel they cannot "bend" or "compromise" to their spouse's view, because it seems to them to be against what "**Hashem's view**" is.

It is therefore necessary that every couple have a family Rav, not only for the purpose of establishing the **halacha** which they follow in practice, but for the purpose of **establishing their Shalom Bayis.**

> The Rav represents for the couple an impartial third

---

49 See Pirkei Avos 5:17: "*Machlokes l'shem Shomayim sofah l'hiskayem*" – "[Any] disagreement that is for the sake of [fulfilling the Will of] Heaven [Hashem], can remain [a disagreement] in the end".

party who is "*Da'as Torah*", who can then render decisions that **both spouses will follow**[50] – even though each partner on their own may have come to a different conclusion than their spouse or to a different conclusion than the Rav.

It follows that once they have chosen a Rav for their family, each partner needs to realize, that even if the Rav decides something that seems to either of them to be totally *opposite* to what is right[51], the act itself of accepting the Rav's *P'sak* (directive) *is the Ratzon Hashem.*

The paradigm example of a couple who disagreed as to what the *Ratzon Hashem* was at a trying time during their lives, was the disagreement between Avraham Avinu and Sarah Emainu in regard to what to do about Yishmael. Sarah noticed how Yishmael was playing with Yitzchak and said that he must be

---

50 The act itself of accepting the Rav's P'sak (directive) *is the Ratzon Hashem.* See Devorim 17: 8–11, where the Torah instructs us that in any case of doubt in regard to fulfilling Hashem's Will in practice, we should go to the Torah Judges of our generation and follow their directives.

51 See Rashi on Devorim 17–11, who quotes Chazal in regard to Halachic decisions of the Sanhedrin, that it is obligatory to follow their Halachic conclusions even when it seems to be *totally opposite* to what is right.

sent out of the house[52]. Rashi[53] describes the type of game that Yishmael would play: "They would go into the field, and he [Yishmael] would take his bow, and shoot at him [Yitzchak] arrows … and he [Yishmael] would say "But I'm just playing" [i.e. "It's only a game"]". Sarah understood clearly, that these are not the type of "games" that Jewish children play; this is something that must be stopped immediately, and should be kept as far away as possible from Yitzchak.

The Torah tells us, that this suggestion was very difficult for Avraham to hear. The Midrash depicts Avraham Avinu's reaction as being: *"How can I send my son away?![54]"*

The "Big – World" View

Avraham, having a man's perspective, was involved his whole life in the larger "world-goal". His constant desire was to bring everyone in the world closer to the knowledge of Hashem[55]. This was a very *"big-picture"* goal, and with that picture in mind Avraham would

---

52 Bereishis 21, 9 – 12.

53 Ibid, 10.

54 Midrash Devorim Rabbah, *parsha daled, os heh.*

55 As the Rambam cites from the Sifri in his Sefer Hamitzvos, Mitzvas Aseh *gimel.*

evaluate everything that came up in his life. When the issue arose regarding Yishmael, it was clear that the best place in the world to experience Hashem's presence was in Avraham's home; everywhere else in the world was rampant with *avodah zarah*.

> From the point of view of Avraham, the decision was clear: "It may be true that Yishmael is not presently acting 'up to par', but maybe with a little more positive influence he'll come around. To throw him out of the house at this point is not even something to be considered; if he has any chance of 'coming around', it is only here in this house". The *"world goal"* of *kiruv* (strengthening others to commitment) was part of Avraham's "bottom-line" decision in regard to Yishmael, who he wanted to be *mekarev* no less than anyone else. This general way of viewing issues comes more naturally to a man, being that he is more prone to thinking about the "bigger picture".

The "Hands – On" Practical View

Sarah on the other hand, took the more *practical* view. "Although it may be that Yishmael's "long-term" future is at stake, we need to focus on what's going on *right now*. Yishmael is not holding where he should be. Every day that he remains in this house and is allowed to play with Yitzchak there is danger involved – both on the physical and spiritual levels. Physically, the games that Yishmael plays are dangerous, and spiritually, through example, Yishmael may influence Yitzchak with his level of behavior. You must separate Yishmael from Yitzchak, and the only way to do it is to send him away".

Only Hashem Could Decide

The issues in this disagreement ran *very* deep. From Avraham's point of view there was *no question* that Yishmael had to stay; from Sarah's point of view there was *no question* that Yishmael had to go. Who could be so all-encompassing to decide between the two logically-valid opinions? The opposing conclusions were so clear to each party and the issues so real, that in this case, only Hashem Himself, *so-to-speak*, could intervene and provide the proper solution.

Hashem said to Avraham, "Whatever Sarah says to you, listen to her voice[56]".

---

56 Bereishis 21:12.

We can't even begin to imagine how hard this must have been for Avraham[57]. Hashem had revealed to him that the real solution and the balance for this situation was the more *practical* view – even though Avraham did not naturally see it that way. To Avraham, sending away his son was the *opposite* of what needed to be done. Nonetheless, he nullified *his own understanding* to accept what Hashem was saying because, ultimately, his goal in life was to do the *Ratzon Hashem*.

An additional Midrash explains even further[58], that not always is the woman's *practical* view the right answer in the situation; but in this specific case, it was. By following his wife's advice, Avraham benefited afterwards tremendously – *on all levels*. Although Yishmael *did* go back to the ways of *avoda zara* when he left Avraham's house[59], the fact that he did not influence Yitzchak or ruin Yitzchak's name in the eyes of others, awarded Avraham Avinu a praise for eternity. All of his offspring who were influenced for life by his

---

57 Sending away Yishmael is counted by many Meforshim as one of the ten trials of Avraham Avinu that are mentioned in Pirkei Avos 5 – 3. See the explanation of Rav Ovadya MiBartenura to that Mishna.

58 Midrash Devorim Rabbah, *parsha daled, os heh.*

59 See Rashi Bereishis 21 – 14.

Torah teachings, remained faithful to his Torah belief and were viewed by the entire world as upstanding people. This then became a proof of validity to the eyes of the entire world for all of the truths that Avraham had been teaching his entire lifetime. In the end, even Yishmael himself did Tshuva before Avraham's passing[60]. So Avraham ended up benefiting on both *the world level* – in regard to his teachings – *and* on *the personal level* – in regard to Yitzchak *and* in regard to Yishmael – by listening to Sarah.

What we see from this, is that *all* men and women, even great Tzaddikim and Tzaddikos, can have two contrasting viewpoints and different ways of looking at things. The *Ratzon Hashem* in such a situation is that they both follow the Torah decision *as rendered by someone who represents to them "Da'as Torah"- their family Rav.*

From this we can learn how important it is for *every* couple to have **an impartial third party whose opinion they both accept without question**, to give them an impartial rendering of the **Ratzon Hashem** in regard to each specific situation[61].

____

60 See Rashi Bereishis 25– 9.

61 In addition, we can also learn from the Parsha of Avraham Avinu, that very

From day one after marriage, if they don't *already* have a Rav they both agree upon, the couple should be making plans to choose a specific Rav for their family[62]. The Rav should be someone who they both feel comfortable speaking to and with whom they each feel can understand *where they are coming from* as individuals, and *where they are going to* – as a couple.

The importance of this in regard to Shalom Bayis cannot be emphasized enough. First of all, it is clear from the words of Chazal in Pirkei Avos that *every person* has an obligation to appoint a Rav for himself:

---

often it is the woman's perspective that is the "right decision" for the situation. Certainly, the ultimate decision that the couple reaches together needs to be one that is thought through and is the balanced and "middle way" for that particular situation (and each particular situation has its own unique balance). But what we can gather from Hashem saying to Avraham "listen to her", is that many times the right answer to a situation will be the one which is the most *practical*. **A man must therefore pay great attention and invest time and thought into understanding his wife's outlook on any given issue. Very often it is that *practical* point of view – which a man tends *not to see* naturally – that holds within it the counterbalance to his "soaring" perspectives, and contains the "down-to-earth" solution that he himself is *really* looking for. It is her perspective that can often add the "Softness" and "Understanding" that is needed within a man's "Strong" approach, to make his abstract goal truly attainable and successful in a practical way.**

62 The couple should not feel that the Rav who they choose right after marriage needs to remain the same Rav for them throughout their entire lives. It is understood that situations change, people move to different communities, etc. and the idea is to choose a Rav who for right now will be the appropriate Halachic authority for them.

"*Aseh Lecha Rav*" (1 – 6, 16)[63]. This is necessary just for technical reasons, because questions can always come up that require more Torah knowledge than either of the spouses may have[64].

But what's more, having a Rav who represents an impartial third party and represents "*Da'as Torah*" in the eyes of the couple, is an invaluable tool for *Shalom Bayis.* Since we learned that real Shalom Bayis takes place when *there **are** differences* and the couple can *bridge the gaps* between them, every couple must have a Rav whose final decisive P'sak they will feel comfortable with – in order to help with bridging the differences in such situations

---

63 It is actually the only directive in the entire Pirkei Avos that is repeated twice in verbatim.

64 The man of the house – although he needs to have some basic knowledge of *halachos* – does not have to be a Rav; so when a question arises that is beyond his realm of knowledge, it is a necessity for him to ask a Rav. Even in a case where the man of the house is himself a Rav, there are numerous *halachic* questions that may come up – whether they be questions pertaining to business, issues with other relatives, issues regarding his position within the community, etc. – that involve him personally; in such cases, Chazal teach us that "*Odom Karov aitzel atzmo*", and he would not be allowed to render the P'sak for himself but would necessarily need to refer the question to another Rav. (Even in a situation where technically one feels "caught" or "cornered", and he just needs a *hashkafic eitza* of how to "get out" of the situation, Chazal teach us that "*Ain chavush matir atzmo m'bais ha'asurim*" – "An imprisoned person cannot take himself out of the jail" (Brachos 5b), and it would be necessary to turn to an additional Rav for the *eitza*).

where the issues are too deep or too involved for them to come to a consensus with.

One or Two Family Rabbonim

Over the years, many students have asked, "Can I have *more than one* Rav?"

> The answer to this question is in Gemara Eiruvin (6b): In regard to *halachah*[65], a person must have *only one* Rav[66].

However, over the years, many students have found it beneficial to find a Rav who will personally guide them in *hashkafah* (Jewish outlook), in addition to *halachah*. Ideally, it is best that the *halachic* Rav be the *hashkafah* and guidance Rav for the family as well. If the couple feels, though, that they both

---

65 This is clearly referring to such *shailos* that require a P'sak based upon *"shikul ha'daas"* – the Rav's weighted decision in a particular situation. If the question is only in regard to verifying information, e.g. what does it say in the Shulchan Aruch, or what is a certain renown Gadol Hador's position on the matter, it is possible to verify by any Rav. Also if there is a technical reason that a different Rav needs to be used, e.g. a chicken needs to be viewed to see whether it is kosher and one's family Rav is out of town , then the question can be asked to a different Rav.

66 The Gemara says: If one follows the opinion of Bais Shamai, he must follow **all** of their opinions – whether they be stringent or lenient; if one follows the opinion of Bais Hillel, he must follow **all** of their opinions – whether they be stringent nor lenient. In *halachah* one must have only one Rav.

relate more to a certain *hashkafic* perspective which is *different* than that of their *halachic* Rav, then I have told students that they may choose a different Rav for *hashkafah* with one condition: If there is ever a contradiction between the *halachic* Rav and the *hashkafic* Rav, they must follow the *halachic* Rav[67]. The *halachah* dictates, that when there is a difference between the opinion of the *halachic* Poskim and the opinion of the *hashkafic* leaders, that we must default to follow the *halachic* view even when lofty considerations are at stake[68].

---

67 This is based upon a P'sak brought in the Mishna Brura in Hilchos Tefillin (Siman 25:42): When there is a contradiction between the *Ba'alei HaKabbalah* and the *halachic* Poskim, it is necessary to follow the *halachic* Poskim. Although the considerations presented by the *Ba'alei HaKabbalah* are certainly very lofty, when this differs with the P'sak of our *halachic* Rav, we need to follow the decision of our personal *halachic* Rav.

68 This is all assuming that the *halachic* Rav has some experiential knowledge as to the background of the couple and as to their present level of connection. Although this factor was generally similar between all couples in previous generations, and so any couple could theoretically ask a *sheilah* of any Rav, today, with the myriad of variables in a Jewish person's life (e.g. a difficult childhood upbringing, a Ba'al/as Tshuva, unique parnassa stresses, etc.), it is not always a given that the Rav who the couple has chosen, will have the experiential knowledge necessary in regard to all the factors in the couple's situation in order to render the appropriate P'sak for their real situation. (To give a superficial example, if a bachur who is 29 years old, a Ba'al Tshuvah of 6 months and English-speaking, decides to accept upon himself as his personal Rav, a Rav from Meah Shearim who has no exposure to any lifestyles outside of that of Meah Shearim, he is likely to receive the wrong Torah

Overall, the benefit of having a Rav who is considered the Rav of the family is invaluable. A couple who makes sure to always maintain a connection with a Rav of their family throughout life's challenging circumstances, will certainly be able to discern over the years how important that connection was in helping them to maintain their Shalom Bayis. Even though nowadays is not always so easy to find a Rav, the couple's persistence and desire to fulfill the directive of "*Aseh lecha Rav*", will undoubtedly pay off over the years.

---

hadrachah (guidance) for himself – and maybe even the wrong *halachic* answers to his *sheilos* – because they are not in proportion according to his true reality.)

Chapter 9

Difference Three: The Action Level – Explosive Energy vs. Stamina

Not only do men and women have different *emotional* expressions and *thought* patterns, but Hashem has also imbued them with different instinctive *abilities* to accomplish their respective goals.

> Since a man must "take on the world", Hashem has equipped him with the innate ability necessary to do so: a burst of **intense energy to conquer** [69] – but one that is short-lived.

---

69 This aspect is mentioned in the Torah narrative regarding the role of a man in the world: "*V'chiv'shuhah*" – "And you shall conquer [the land]" (Breishis 1;28). In regard to a man's role in the *tikun* (correction) of the world, the word "conquer" is specifically emphasized. The natural quality of a man is that he has the energy and strength to take on world challenges in a way that he can successfully conquer them.

Since a woman must tend to the needs of her home
with consistency, Hashem has equipped her with the
innate ability necessary to do so: a slower *long-lasting
energy called "**stamina**"*, which gives her the ability to
deal with the constant successive challenges of the
home[70].

> In order to bridge over this contrast in the nature
> of their energies, both spouses must be aware from
> the onset, that when it comes to dealing with any
> situation that requires *taking action*, their natural
> tendencies *will be opposite.*

While a man's unique quality allows him to "take-
off" from his home and to "take on the world" in
an explosive and intense way (e.g. in the form of
arguing his point in a *sugya* [section of Torah legal
discussion] or in securing a business deal, etc.), a
woman's unique quality allows her to fortify the
"home base" and to draw from her long-lasting
energy to constantly shift successfully from one

---

70 This aspect is mentioned in the Torah narrative regarding the role of a woman
in the world: *"Aim kol chai"* – "The mother of all [that will come to] life" (Breishis
3:20). In regard to the woman's role in the *tikun* (correction) of the world, the
words "mother of all [that will come to] life" are specifically emphasized. The
natural quality of a "mother" is *to be constantly "there" and available* to fill the needs
of her children who she brings to life.

challenge into the next and to create *a place* that gives
a constant feel of *security and nurturing.*

> After the whole day of being outside, once a man
> has spent his energy at completing his goals and
> he finally arrives home, he is often *totally* exhausted
> without the strength to take on even one additional
> chore. In contrast, a woman, even after a long day,
> can generally still find the energy within herself to
> shift into yet *another* challenge and to deal with it
> successfully until its completion[71].

A rocket ship cannot fly without a base. Its entire
existence in "outer-space" is limited, if it cannot
return to its home base.

> As husband and children "take-off" daily on their
> various paths into the "outer" world, their successes will
> be directly dependent upon the *love and support* that
> they feel from their home base. That base is *the woman*[72].

---

71 This does not mean to imply that women never get tired. The statement that is
suggested here is made only for the purpose of bringing out the contrast of *kochos*
(*natural strengths*): a woman's ability to continue to endure many more challenges
throughout the day, in comparison to a man's ability to invest his *kochos* strongly
into a certain number of undertakings and then be apt to "shut-down" completely,
accents the contrast between the natural "explosive energy" of a man vs. the natural
"stamina" of a woman.

72 The Gemara (Shabbos 118b) relates that Rabbi Yosi would not call his wife
"my wife" but rather "my home". From Rashi it is clear (ibid) that Rabbi Yosi's intent

Although the reality of the woman being "the home base" may sound like a relatively simple idea, in practice it works on a very deep psychological level. The added surge of *kochos* (strength) and the ability to accomplish in the world that a man feels after getting married, can be directly attributed to this single factor. The fact that a man knows **that he has someone behind him** who is waiting for him at home and who is "rooting" for his successes outside, motivates him with an instinctive boost of energy, *like the fuel which drives a rocket ship.*

> Therefore, a woman should never minimize the importance of her position as the basis of the home. Although everything in the house may seem more consistent and less "exciting" than all of those challenging situations going on outside, it is precisely that consistency and security *that she offers* which is what empowers the members of her family to perform their best.

---

was to internalize the message that "his wife *is* the home" – she is the focal point of the home that everything else revolves around. We tend to think that a home is defined by four walls, and that even if someone "comes home" to a room where there is no one waiting, it is still considered a home. The Gemara teaches us, that **the main part of the home that a person "comes home to", is the *person* who is there waiting to receive everyone who comes. That person is the woman.**

Chapter 10

Difference Four: The "Needs" Level – Support vs. Recognition

What motivates and "fuels" a man the most, is when he intuitively feels his wife's **support**.

> The greatest contribution that a woman can offer towards the building of the home, is the *support* that she shows each and every one of her family members; whether it be through the **technical assistance** she extends, the **compassion and concern** that she exhibits, or, most importantly, the **belief that she has in their abilities to succeed** – even if that belief remains unspoken.

When husband and children "take off" daily on their various paths, she already paves the way for their successes by preparing the provisions they need, escorting them on their way with her smiling blessings, and by giving them the intuitive sense that *they will be successful,* through **her unspoken belief in them.**

> The world outside is a rough place, and those who "go out" and struggle to swim in its waves, often come back battered and exhausted by the end of the day, having been pushed or even shattered – physically, emotionally or psychologically.

The place to "recharge one's batteries" in order to be able to face the next day, is in the place called "home" – by the person called "home"[73] – and the "recharger" is that implicit wave of unwavering *support* that the woman of the house exudes.

> But to be a 24 hour-a-day support system, is not possible without being filled with some source of energy. Thus, a woman herself has a very real need – as different than that of a man – to be **recognized.**

Whereas a man can forgo and even ignore recognition from his peers, a woman cannot properly continue her job in the home without *recognition* from her husband – *even for one day.*

---

73 See footnote 72.

> Being aware of this difference, that a man's greatest
> need is for "*support*" and a woman's greatest need
> is for "*recognition*", can help us bridge over the gaps
> by giving our spouses what *they* need – not what we
> ourselves feel what *we* need.

Since a man does not have a strong need for
recognition, it is hard for him to realize its necessity.
However, once a man begins to work on "*giving
recognition*", he will be surprised to see how many
doors of light and happiness it opens up in his wife's
heart, creating positivity in the home, and ultimately
bringing him to feel those same feelings as well.

> Being that a man is not used to doing this naturally,
> initially he needs to invest time and effort at practicing
> various ways of how to *show recognition* to his wife, until
> such time that it actually becomes a part of his nature.
> See Chapter 11 for advice on how to do this.

Since a woman's need for "*recognition*" is intuitively
translated to her as "*support*", it is likely that it will
be hard for her to understand the need that her
husband has to receive her "*support*" - when it comes
as unconnected to "*recognition*"[74]. However, once a

---

74 For example, when a woman is talking to a friend and receives *recognition* in
the conversation by hearing that her feelings were validated by her friend, she feels

woman begins to work on "*giving support*", she will be surprised to see how many doors of light and happiness it opens up in her husband's heart, creating positivity in the home, and ultimately bringing her to feel those same feelings as well.

> Being that a woman is not used to doing this naturally, initially she needs to invest time and effort at practicing various ways of how to *show support* to her husband, until such time that it actually becomes part of her nature. See Chapter 12 for advice on how to do this.

---

satisfied and empowered, and therefore does not generally require any *added support* by the fact that someone has now prepared a supper for her (it is "nice", but not a necessity). However, when a man comes home after a day of wrestling with the world – and especially after a day that included failures – he *does not* have a need at all for the *recognition* of his efforts through talking about it, but he *does* have a very real need to *feel supported* after his failure. This *support* is indicated to him through the fact that someone has prepared a supper for him; the message of which he receives clearly and feels satisfied and empowered with – even without exchanging *any words at all*.

Chapter 11

Tips for a Man to Work on Showing Recognition

Here are some practical ways that a man can work on showing *recognition* for his wife:

1. Expressing appreciation for what has been done;
2. Staying in touch when away;
3. Remembering at special times such as birthdays, anniversaries, etc.;
4. Noticing and complimenting change;
5. Knowing wife's tastes of food or items that *she* likes to buy, and occasionally buying her a gift that *she* likes – for no special reason at all;
6. Sacrificing quality time.
7. Asking his wife what she needs or offering to help when she is in a time of distress.

8. Most important, to be "*A listening ear*". Just because a woman runs a major support system, her needs to be comforted and heard are no less than anyone else's.

> To sum up, a man must communicate – almost constantly – through his actions and words, that he **cares** and that he **recognizes** that there is someone "behind him" who is giving of herself *to support him*.

1. Expressing appreciation for what has been done.
> **Note to husband:** When you arrive home after a long day, it is natural for you not to notice anything other than your supper. If you follow your instincts, and the first thing you ask about when you walk through the door is: "What's for supper?", then you will be giving the unspoken message to your wife of: "*Nothing that you did today has any importance to me. What's important to me is to satisfy **my** hunger.*" By inquiring first and foremost about the food that *you* need, you are indirectly giving a message to your wife that anything else does not register as making any difference to you at all. When "translated" into your wife's "language" that means to her: "*Everything that you did the entire day in the house – to work so hard and make it so beautiful – is worth nothing to me*". This is crushing for a woman – even though you may not understand her devastated

reaction to your question. "Why is she so upset? All I did was walk into the house and ask: 'What's for supper?'"

On the other hand, if you practice shifting your focus when you walk into the house to concentrate on *your wife's needs*, and you accustom yourself to expressing **sincere recognition and value for her accomplishments** of the day, for example: "Wow, this room looks amazing!" or "The bookcase is so clean!" etc., – then you will probably sense an atmosphere of happiness and satisfaction in your home, that will give your wife the added motivation she needs in order to serve you that supper that you were waiting for and to give you all of the support that you need, in an even greater way.

2. Staying in touch when away.

Even more important than the topic of discussion during the phone call, is just *the fact that you called home.* The call itself indicates to your wife, that you **recognize** that there is someone there at home waiting for you.

3. Remembering at special times such as birthdays, anniversaries, etc.

Even more important than the type of card or

present that you buy for the occasion, is *the fact that you actually remembered the date* (if you can remember it on your own without being told, it's even more praiseworthy). The fact that you actually gave importance to the day that she came into your life, shows your wife in an unspoken way, that you **recognize the importance and value of who *she* is** – the importance and value of that unique, additional *neshama* (soul) whom Hashem has brought into the world and into your life for *your* benefit.

4. Noticing and complimenting *change.*

Although by nature you may not pay so much attention as to the order of the family pictures on the living room wall[75], or to the fancy quiche that was prepared as a side dish instead of the regular canned vegetables, try your best to *notice and appreciate change.* This shows **recognition for the time and thought** that your wife invested into her undertaking for that day.

---

75 From a man's point of view, I know that you are probably thinking: "What difference could it possibly make whether the picture in the living room is hanging on the right wall or on the left wall?" But, regarding this, my Rebbe in Mussar Rav Wolbe *z"l* said: It is known that the Holy *Shechina* rests upon a Jewish home (Sefer Tomer Dvorah). When a woman changes the place of a picture on the wall in order to position it in the most beautiful place for it in that room, it is actually considered as the same spiritual level as the holy level of *Mekashet es HaShechina* (Adorning of the Holy *Shechina*).

The most direct way to show that you recognize your
wife's efforts to please you is to offer compliments.
Every compliment is a clear expression of
recognition for your wife. Compliments are
therefore an *indispensable tool* for building Shalom
Bayis, and should be used as often as possible – but
with the condition that you can say them *sincerely*.

> **Note to husband:** The goal is not to say as many
> compliments as possible; the goal is to say them
> *sincerely*. Often times, it is even possible to express
> sincere *appreciation and recognition* for something
> that has been done, *even without using any words*. For
> example, practice showing appreciation with your
> hands like showing a sign of a "thumbs-up". Also
> practice at just using the exclamations "Wow!" or
> "Psssssss …" at something that your wife did, even
> without adding any further explanation.
>
> You will quickly come to realize, that if a compliment
> or feeling that you expresses is being said **sincerely**, no
> times are too many.

**5. Knowing wife's tastes of food or items that *she*
likes to buy, and occasionally buying her a gift that
she likes – for no special reason at all.**

If you start to take notice, you will see that many

people generally choose something that **they themselves** like when buying gifts for others – even though it could be that the person whom they are buying it for will not really like it at all. When buying a present for your wife, you will award her the greatest *recognition* and thus give her the greatest satisfaction, if you buy her something that **she** likes. Just the fact that you took out the time and interest *to learn what **she** likes,* gives your wife the unspoken message that you **recognize and value** who she is.

An additional element of *recognition* is relayed when you occasionally buy her a gift *for no special reason at all.* Since you have no reason to get her the gift other than to show her that you *recognize* her intrinsic importance at every moment, that itself is one of the greatest **statements of recognition** to your wife that you can make[76]. If you get it wrapped, or buy a special

---

76 This type of present also has extra importance because it is not being forced upon the *giver* in any way. When the *giving* is done because one spouse "has to" (for example, when that spouse has already learnt from the results of past experiences that they had "better not" miss a birthday), then its value of being given sincerely for the recognition of the spouse is greatly diminished. The Gemara Yerushalmi (Peah 3b) relates two varied incidents of Kibud Av: In the one case a son would prepare kingly delicacies for his father, but when presenting it to him would put it down with a throw, ordering him to eat it, like one would talk to a dog. In the second case, the military wanted to draft the father, and the son, whose work was to turn a heavy millstone for hours every day, said to his father: "Father, you stay here and turn the millstone and I

card, or add flowers (or all three together), you will be opening wellsprings of positivity and happiness in your wife's heart, because each of these acts shows a unique level of added *recognition*[77].

6. Sacrificing quality time.

Note to husband: This does not include those times when you "allow" your wife to speak to you – for example, *while* you are eating – because that is not considered "quality" time. "Quality time" means,

---

will go instead of you to the army". The Gemara concludes by declaring that the first son received Gehenom in retribution for his "giving", and the second son received Gan Eden as payment for giving his father the job of forced labor. It is clear from this Gemara that **the value of the present itself is not what determines the greatness of the present, but rather** *the way that it is given.*

77 I once asked a student: "Do you know why women like flowers so much? After all, it's quite an extra cost on your budget (for a really nice bouquet), and they die after two days anyway. How much of a difference could they really make?" I explained to him that the answer is: "Specifically for that reason, is *why* flowers are so important to a woman; *because* they cost so much, and *because* they die after two days, and you *still* bought them *for her*! Because you *recognize* her importance to you, you're willing to do something *for her* which has no importance for you as a man (or is even a loss)!! That's why buying flowers at special times is so important. And it's the same with the gift wrapping or buying a nice card. From your side, you could have accomplished giving the gift by just presenting it without any wrapping, or you could have just scribbled some words on a paper and given it to your wife without having to spend money on a card. It must be that you went through that effort and spent that money because you *recognize* your wife's importance. And you'll notice, that if you scribbled a few words on a piece of paper, it's likely it will get thrown out; but if buy your wife a card and write even less (just something affectionate and sign your name), it's likely that you will find it stored neatly away in her drawer – for years and years afterwards."

when it comes off of time *that is of quality to you.* Example: You were planning to leave the house for something important *to you* – e.g. to learn, to work, or to go meet friends – and after sensing that your wife really needs to talk, you pushed off your own appointment for a while. That is what sacrificing "quality time" means. By doing so you show your wife that you **recognize** the importance of her needs.

7. Asking wife what she needs or offering to help when she is in a time of distress.

When you see that your wife is really in distress about something but *is not expressing her feelings,* show an interest to know what she's feeling; or, better yet, ask her if you could make her a hot drink or something to eat[78].

The female emotional system is such, that a woman is *always* looking for someone to share her emotions with. Especially in situations that are really trying, she feels an extra strong need to "unload" and to share what she's feeling with someone else. Naturally her first and best choice of who to share it with is her husband. However, sometimes the "volume" of

---

78 Rabbi Simcha Cohen, Habayis Hayehudi, Part 2, p.210.

her feelings is running so high, that she can't even imagine "unloading" all of this onto her husband; it seems almost unfair to do to him. She then ends up "holding in" all those feelings, which can cause her to feel very upset, or paralyzed, or to find herself in a situation of internal turmoil. At that time, even in her "wildest dreams", she cannot imagine that her husband would be willing to listen to her.

> *Recognition* means that *I value who you are, as you are* – no matter when or what situation you are going through. It is specifically at those times, when your wife seems to be closed up or lost in her tornado of emotions, that you can show **recognition** – just by acknowledging that "*I see what you're going through and I know that it's hard.*" Even a deeper message of recognition is relayed when a man doesn't actually say those words, he just thinks them and says instead: "Wow, you look like you've really had a hard day. Can I make you a hot tea or get you something to eat?"

8. Most important, to be "A listening ear".
   Often you will find, that even without offering any actual solution to the problem, a lot of tension will be reduced just by the fact that *you listened.*

Rav Wolbe *z"l* taught us, that the greatest *chesed* (act

of lovingkindness) that a person can do is what
is described in the Mishna in Pirkei Avos (6:6):
"Nosei b'ol im chaveiro" – carrying the yoke of a
friend *together* with him[79]. He explained that any
person who finds himself in a situation of suffering,
undergoes an additional pain of *"being alone"* in his
suffering. He went on to say, that this additional pain
of loneliness causes even greater emotional pain
than the pain from the predicament itself. When
a friend comes by to inquire about the situation,
as in the Mitzva of Bikur Cholim, what he does in
effect, is that he breaks into that "bubble of solitude"
surrounding his friend, and thus relieves him from a
major part of the discomfort he is feeling[80].

> This rule applies between a husband and wife as
> well. Just by being "a listening ear", a husband can
> fulfill his part in being **"Nosei B'ol Im Chaveiro"**
> every day – by "carrying" the emotional pain of the
> situations that his wife has experienced, *together with
> her* – and thus he can give her one of the greatest gifts

---

79 Sefer Alei Shur, *Chelek Alef, Sha'ar Rishon, Perek Shivii.*

80 Sefer Alei Shur, Chelek Alef, *Mavo L'Sha'ar HaRevii.* This can also be understood
to be the intent in the words of Chazal that "One who visits a friend who is sick,
removes one-sixtieth of his pain from him" (Nedarim 39b).

that she could ever ask for. The fact that he listens to her *actively*[81] and that he allows her to share her feelings [*and then validates them*[82] – see footnote], is

---

81 "Active listening" is a form of listening that shows occasional participation from the listener, such as facial expressions that change according to what is being described in the story, occasional vocal reactions (such as "wow!", "I can't believe it", "ugh", "oy", clicking of tongue 2–3 times, etc.), and occasional gesticulation (such as lifting hands to face, putting one hand on heart, etc.); all this is in contrast to "passive listening," where the storyteller has no indication as to what the listener thinks of his story.

82   When a person expresses an experience to another, especially if it's an "emotionally loaded" experience, what he's really looking for more than anything is that the listener understand *his emotions*. What he's *not* especially looking for is that the listener, record and retain all *the technical details* of his story. So if you're naturally a more intellectual listener, try and practice to "listen emotionally".
What "listening emotionally" means, is that you are able to grasp the *feeling* that is being conveyed while you listen. To "listen emotionally" is when you *don't* listen so carefully to every detail, but your heart is instead focused upon listening extra carefully to try and identify *the emotion being described.*
To give a regular 'everyday' example of "emotional listening", imagine that 'Mommy' is telling her spouse that in the morning the bus-driver picked up the kids late, and because of that she was late in taking 'the little one' to playgroup, and because of that the kids in playgroup had already started their 'activities' by the time she came, and because of that none of the 'assistants' could come to answer the door, and because of that the organizer of playgroup *herself* came to the door, and because of that she reminded mother that the family hasn't paid yet for last month, and because she didn't have any money with her she was *terribly embarrassed* – what her spouse should *not answer* is: "What a terrible bus driver – he's always so late!"
His wife's point in telling the story was not about the technicalities; for someone who is used to "listening emotionally", it was clearly about her emotions. He should therefore try to use the time – while still in the midst of listening to the story – to formulate the appropriate word in his mind to describe *the emotion* that he hears her expressing (for example: upset, frustrated, pressured, embarrassed). Then when she finishes her recounting of what took place, he should answer her immediately only

> one of the greatest acts of showing **recognition** for his wife that he can perform.

Just start today to work on one or two of the categories that were mentioned. Remember: "Practice Makes Perfect". Certainty over time your actions will make a noticeable difference to your wife – which she will *tremendously* appreciate – even if you never did so until today.

---

with *that exact word*: "Wow, you must have felt *sooo embarrassed*!!"
This is called "mirroring emotions". It's when you give back to the person telling the story, the *emotion* that he just expressed in the form of a word. What it does, is that it shows the storyteller that you "got him"; you *really* understood what he was trying to convey. And that experience of feeling "*really understood*" (emotionally!) is from the most validating experiences possible and is a major form of showing *recognition* from a man towards his wife.

Chapter 12

Tips for a Woman to Work on Showing Support

When husband and children "touch base" and return home, she is there:

With a smile to greet them;

With pleasant words of greeting;

With food, when necessary;

With a neat room;

With a listening ear.

Most importantly, with some encouraging words, and to voice that *she* is happy and satisfied with their efforts.

Sometimes by just saying the words: "We know that it's all from Hashem; but no matter what, *I believe in you*" – a woman can notice massive amounts of tension fading away from her husband's face.

What is the Merit of Women

There is a well-known Gemara in Brachos[83] which asks the question: "With what [specific acts] do women *merit* [to receive such a unique level of reward in the future – that is even greater than that of the men themselves [84]]?"

> The Gemara answers that women receive such special reward by virtue of the fact that they take their children to the shul (where the children used to learn), and that they allow their husbands to go to learn and wait for them until they return home.

On a superficial level, the merits mentioned in this answer don't seem to warrant such a reward that is even greater than that of the men themselves (who actually do the learning). Why would the fact that the women physically lead their children to their place of study and wait for their husbands until they return home be *so* praiseworthy as to merit such a distinctive level in the world to come?

> Once we understand the major contribution that

---

83 17 a.

84 As is indicated from the words of the Navi Yeshiyahu, 3:9; see Rashi, Brachos 17a, piece beginning *"Gedolah havtachah"*.

a woman makes to all the members of her family by being the *support* of her home, this Gemara can be readily understood. It comes to teach us that a woman's *support* can profoundly affect the members of her family in the *deepest* ways. Here are some examples:

1. When a woman escorts her child to his place of learning *with her smiling countenance* – **she has already assured his success** at being able to learn and to retain what he is taught. Due to the positive self-image that he receives from her, he will be more prone to feeling good about himself and to relating to his Torah learning as a *positive* experience.

When a woman sends off her husband *with the feeling that she is supportive* of what he is doing, and when she provides an accepting and encouraging environment to return home to – **she has already assured his success** during the interim time that he spends learning. Due to the positivity he receives from her, he will be more prone to relating to his Torah learning as a *positive* experience. In the future it will become clear that the cause of the childrens' and her husband's successes, was the woman of the house and *the feel that she gave them.* Therefore, her reward will be even greater than that of the men themselves.

    2. This does not only apply when everything in life is going "as planned". An even greater aspect of *support* that a woman shows for her husband is when things are not going so well.

Being "*supportive*" means to "root" for her husband's success and well-being, *even when the times are rough.* When she can reaffirm her belief in her husband's ability - even when he is going through a difficult time and has not been successful at procuring his goals, she is following in the path of those women who are designated to receive *the greatest reward* which is set aside specifically for the women in the future.

    3. Since a man was created as being naturally "*stronger*" and to be a *mashpia* ("*giver*") for his wife, he has a very real emotional need to feel that his wife is happy in life **because of him**[85]. When a woman uses her being naturally "*softer*" than a man to show her husband that she is happy and satisfied with what he provides for her[86], she thus fills a very real need that

---

85 Habayis Hayehudi, Part 2, pg. 17.

86 This is assuming that her husband is actually providing for her in a reasonable fashion. In a case where the husband is clearly providing in a deficient fashion, it is necessary to consult what sooner with the Rav of the family so that he can guide the

her husband has, which only strengthens their bond as a couple. Most certainly a woman *should not use her natural quality of being "soft" as a reason not to show any appreciation* about what her husband does for her[87], because that would serve only to weaken their bond as a couple. Rather, *she should value and listen to his challenges* as if they are the trials he is enduring in order to fill *her* needs.

By being open to listen and accepting of what her husband has to say rather than being demanding of him, she fills a very deep need that he has.

Just start today to work on one or two of the categories that were mentioned. Remember: "Practice Makes Perfect". Certainty over time your actions will make a noticeable difference to your husband – which he will *tremendously* appreciate – even if you never did so until today.

---

husband to fulfill his obligations to the family in a reasonable and accepted manner.

87 The more that a woman can focus on *valuing* what her husband does do for her and on sending him a clear message that *she appreciates* what he provides for her, will not only add strength to the couple's bond, but will naturally cause the husband to want to care even more for his wife's needs. If a woman does not show any true feelings of appreciation *for what her husband **does** provide,* it will only serve to weaken the couple's bond, and to naturally cause the husband to feel like a failure in the area that he has a need most to succeed in – namely, to feel that his wife is truly happy and satisfied *because of him.*

Chapter 13

Making Your Spouse "Number One"

Being aware of the contrasting traits and needs that men and women are designed with, will help us to be better equipped to fill those particular needs when they arise. We may now have tools to "bridge over the differences" when they arise and thus to allow for Shalom to reign in our Bayis.

> However, beyond just avoiding the points of difference and maintaining an atmosphere of Shalom, there is an *ultimate level* of unity in marriage toward which every couple should strive for. This unity can come about only once we work on keeping the Shalom in our Bayis and on "bridging the gaps" for a prolonged amount of time.

The ultimate level of **giving** from a woman to her

husband is when she can give him her **support** in a
way where he is "**Number 1**" to her.

> The ultimate level of *giving* from a man to his wife is
> when he can give her his *recognition* in a way where
> she is "**Number 1**" to him.

The main effort required to reach these ultimate
levels of *giving* and *unity*, is to work on your *mind-set*.
This means that you may need to learn to focus on all
the *positive* attributes of your spouse[88] and to accept
even the ungifted, incomplete parts of them, as being
part of the "package" that is best *for you*[89].

> According to Hashem's **hashgachah**, your spouse
> *really is* Number One for you.

Begin to *think, say* to your spouse, and *feel*: "You are
the Greatest One in the World *for me*".

> Once you start to *feel* in your heart that your spouse
> *really is* the greatest in the world for you – *your spouse*
> *will also start to feel toward you* those same feelings that
> you feel about them as well[90].

---

88 Everyone in the world has some unique innate positive attributes (see Alei
Shur, *Chelek Alef*, p. 146.) See also footnote 98.

89 To help *you* to accomplish *your tikun* in this world.

90 Shlomo Hamelech teaches us in Mishlei (27:19): "*K'mayim hapanim l'panim*" –
"Like the water [which reflects back] the face of a person, to the person [himself]",

Although all of this may sound simple, the level we are now discussing really involves the work of a lifetime. The levels of unity that are included under the heading of "Shalom Bayis" are like the rungs of a ladder; they ascend constantly higher and higher. The **avoda** (spiritual task) of each couple is to continue climbing that ladder throughout their lifetime. Each successive rung that either spouse is able to advance, even if seemingly minute, is really another *huge* step forward toward attaining the ultimate levels of unity that are included under the heading of "Shalom Bayis".

> We have learned that the main quality that a man needs to receive from his wife is her "*support*"[91], and that the main quality a woman needs to receive from her husband is his "*recognition*"[92].

While a chasan or kallah who has *just begun* to work on *giving* to their spouse what their spouse needs, will already notice (with Hashem's help) much change

---

"*kain lev ha'adam l'adam*" – "so too is the heart of one man to another". The heart emotion that you reveal toward another person will always be "reflected back", and will cause an arousal of those same emotions that you are radiating from yourself,, to be aroused in their heart as well.

91 See Chapter 12.

92 See Chapter 11.

for the better, the *ultimate levels* of "Shalom Bayis" come only when each spouse practices to reach the "**ultimate level**" of *giving* support or recognition to their spouse.

My Husband – The "Number 1" Man to Support

The "ultimate level" of what a man is looking to receive from his wife is her *support* in a way that **he is "Number 1" to her.**

> It is not necessary for him to be considered the truly ABSOLUTE "Number 1" man in the world – because by definition no such thing is possible (for every man in the world to "really" be "Number 1" would be mutually exclusive). Rather, what **is** necessary, is that he be considered the *absolute* "Number 1" man **in his wife's eyes.** He wants *her* to believe in him in a way that his accomplishments will be *the most meaningful and most successful in the world* **to her**. For a woman to give her husband this level of support means that she has to train herself to **sincerely feel** that her husband's plan of action in life – in her eyes – is better than that of anyone else's in the world.

As hard as this may sound, it is really not so far beyond what a woman is doing already. Every woman who marries, in essence, has already made an implicit statement that this man that she has agreed to marry, **is the one** who she is willing to sacrifice for and support *more than any other man in the world*[93]. This implicit statement already includes the notion, that she trusts her husband's understanding to the point where she is willing to commit herself to him, more than to anyone else in the entire world.

> The goal in Shalom Bayis, then, would be to actualize that implicit commitment, to the point where it becomes extremely clear to her husband, that she sincerely feels *on an internal level,* that from her point of view, his plans are better *for her* than anyone else's in the entire world.

My Wife – The "Number 1" Woman to Recognize

The "ultimate level" of what a woman is looking to receive from her husband, is his *recognition* in a way that **she is "Number 1" to him.**

---

93 The Ra"n (one of the Rishonim in Gemara Nedarim), in his explanation of the "mechanics" of how the act of Kiddushin works from the Torah, explains that by accepting the gift of monetary value that the man offers her (after pronouncing the words *"harai at mekudeshes"* etc.), the woman is in effect making a statement of *nullification of her will to the will of her husband,* and this is how the husband has the ability to make the acquisition of Kiddushin (Nedarim 40a, piece beginning *V'Isha.*)

It is not necessary for her to be the truly ABSOLUTE "Number 1" woman at all the praiseworthy characteristics of a woman in the world – because by definition no such thing is possible (for every woman in the world to "really" be "Number 1" would be mutually exclusive). Rather, what **is** necessary is that she be considered the "Number 1" person to be recognized and valued as a woman **to him.** For a man to give his wife this level of recognition means that he has to train himself to **sense sincerely,** that his wife's positive attributes as a woman – in his eyes – are greater than that of anyone else's in the entire world.

As hard as this may sound, it is really not so far beyond what a man is doing already. Every man who marries has already in essence made an implicit statement that this woman that he has chosen to marry, **is the one** who he recognizes as having the greatest overall level of womanly characteristics for him in the world[94]. This

---

94 Being that a man can marry only one woman, the man is in effect *making a statement* that this woman whom he has chosen to marry, is that woman who, through her unique attributes, he can grow with and best reach his completion, more than with any other woman in the world. Even if the *hashgachah* that brought about the marriage of the couple took place in a way that seemed not to be their choice, since we believe in *hashgachah pratis,* we are to assume that this **really is** the woman or the man that is best as a spouse to grow with and to reach completion with, more than with anyone else in the world (unless it is *clearly* evident otherwise – but this requires

implicit statement already includes the notion that he recognizes **this** woman's attributes to the point where he is willing to choose her for himself as his wife, above anyone else in the entire world[95].

> The goal in Shalom Bayis, then, would be to actualize that statement which is implicit in his choice, to the point where it becomes extremely clear to his wife, that he sincerely feels *on an internal level,* that in his mind her unique "package" of positive womanly attributes, when considered all together, is the best "package" of womanly attributes for him in the world.

All of this takes work. The main effort required is

---

the help of a third party, who is an outside source, to determine; see footnote 126).

95 Even according to Torah law that a man can marry more than one wife, this premise still holds true: The reason for a man being able to marry more than one wife, is based upon the deeper meaning in the makeup of Yaakov Avinu's household; namely, that each one of Yaakov's wives had a specific aspect to help him reach completion in. This is based upon the reality of their *shoresh neshamos* and the realities of the spiritual levels above. In the time of the giving of the Torah, in times when the spiritual realities and *tikun* of each person were more evident, a man would be able to marry a number of wives in order that each one help him to perform his *tikun* in one *specific* area from among those that his *neshama* needed to correct on the spiritual plane. However, our ability to access this knowledge of the spiritual realms has greatly diminished over the years, and has certainly not been clear enough to warrant a man to marry more than one wife since the time of *Rabbenu Gershom* (approx. 1000 years ago). In any case, it is clear that the fact that a man may marry numerous wives according to Torah law still does not negate the basic premise of each woman being *the most important in the world for that man* in the area that she helps him in to reach his *tikun.*

essentially to work on your **mind-set**. Everyone knows that if they were standing in the place of Adam Harishon and Chava, where all that existed in the world was only one representative of each gender, this mind-set would come naturally. The problem is that we live today in a world where there seem to be so many people to choose from, and we can get very confused as to whether the one that we've actually chosen is really that one who is "the Number 1 person" for us in the world.

In Truth Your Spouse Really Is Number One for You

This necessitates that we reiterate one of the most fundamental principles of Torah belief, *Hashgachah Pratis* (Specific Heavenly Providence). If we really believe that Hashem runs everything in the world in a way that goes even beyond our free choice[96], we must believe that the person with whom Hashem has brought each of us together with – respectively – and

---

96 See Chovos Halevavos, Sha'ar Avodas Elokim, *perek zayin*, that although we in our finite minds cannot grasp how *Hashem's Foreknowledge* and our total *free choice* can be coexistent, our belief according to the Torah is that they both exist simultaneously – all of the time. Therefore, although each person exercises his *free choice* when choosing a spouse, this does not negate the fact that simultaneously it was Hashem's *hashgachah pratis* and Foresight **as well,** that lead to the marriage of any two individuals.

who He has ultimately united us with, is exactly that person who will bring us to our greatest level of *tikun* and completion in our worship of Hashem in this lifetime. Although there may be work to face, we must view this as our personal challenge and [at the same time as our personal *opportunity*] to reach each of *our* unique potential in our personal *avodas* Hashem.

And so if our goal in marriage is really a spiritual one, and we believe that the person who the events of *hashgachah* has united us with, *is really* that person who is *most fitting* to help us to reach that goal, then the effort and internal work will just come naturally. Very often, deep down, we *do* know that the person we are married to *really is* that person who can bring us to reach the highest levels we can reach of connection to Hashem – if only we could live with them in harmony. Just that very often what faces us is the decision whether or not *to invest committed effort* to merit that harmony. When we merit to actually do the work, it begins to become clearer and clearer that the spouse who I am married to is truly *that specific neshama* who can bring **me** to the *greatest* level – both physically and spiritually – that *I* am expected to get to.

Think, Say and Feel: "You Are the Greatest One in the World for Me"

On a practical level, there are some "hands-on" tools that we can already utilize in order to help us in this climb toward making our spouse "Number 1" for us:

1. Spend time *thinking* about the idea: *Channel* your energies and desires into the one person who Hashem has brought you together with – **as if** there were no other person of that gender in the entire world.

2. Begin to ***say and express*** openly to your spouse how you much value *their* unique strengths – on all levels: intellectual, emotional and physical. Everyone in the world has unique G-dly abilities that they were blessed with more than anyone else[97]. Put in time to think about, to define and to describe what unique positive attributes it is that your spouse has, and make an effort to praise them verbally for it[98].

3. Once you start to *speak* about it more, the path will be open for you to actually ***feel and appreciate*** those unique strengths of your spouse. Once you start to feel in your heart that your spouse *really is the*

---

97 See footnote 88.

98 For help with identifying your spouse's unique positive traits, see the list of positive character traits in Appendix 2.

greatest in the world for you, no doubt that your spouse will start to feel towards you the same way as well[99]; your commitment to them will naturally bring them to commit to you. You will be *giving* your spouse on a sincere heart level what he/she *truly needs* [full **support** or full **recognition**], and that should bring them in return to naturally *give back* to you whatever *you* *need* on a sincere heart level.

By realizing that achieving Shalom Bayis is an ongoing process (similar to other areas of growth in life that we aspire to reach in our *avodas* Hashem), we can consistently grow throughout life in our quest toward the **ultimate level** of connection in marriage. Once I can sincerely live with and feel at all times, that the spouse that Hashem has given me, *is* **the Number 1 person in the world** who can help *me* to reach all of *my* unique potential in this lifetime, **then I have truly transformed my** "*Me*" **into being a** "*We*".

---

99 See footnote 90.

Chapter 14

Communications – the Key to Bridging Differences

Now that we are aware of general differences that exist between all men and women, we can try our best to bridge those differences when they arise and to create Shalom in our Bayis, with Hashem's help. However, those keys of understanding cannot yet open the "lock of solitude" without one imperative ingredient: **Communication.**

> **Communication** is the key that **must** be used to be successful at bridging the differences.

A lack of communication is the first and foremost cause of an impending severance, **chas v'shalom.**

> If you want to separate any two people – make sure they don't communicate.

I once heard from the renowned *Mechanech* Rabbi Zecharya Greenwald *shlita,* a beautiful, eye-opening explanation based on teachings from our Rebbe in mussar Rabbi Shlomo Wolbe *z"l:*

The Torah relates to us that the *Dor Haflagah* received the punishment of being spread throughout the world because of their transgressions. The pasuk reads: "Hashem said, 'Behold it is one nation and one language for all, and this has caused them to do [what they did]; and now, nothing will stand in their way [to accomplish] whatever they decide to do. Let us go down [there] and confuse their languages, so that they should not understand one another's language. And Hashem dispersed them from there over the face of the whole earth"[100].

We know that Hashem could do anything. If Hashem's intent was just to separate the people one from another so that they would cease building the *migdal* [tower], why couldn't He just make a *nes* [miracle] that would cause the people to instantaneously find themselves in different parts of the world? Why was it necessary for Hashem to first confuse their languages and *only then* bring about the

---

100 Breishis 11 – 6–8.

spreading of the people throughout the world?

What the Torah is teaching us is an outstanding lesson regarding the power of *communication*: "**Behold it** is one nation and one language for all, and this has caused them to do [what they did]; and now, *nothing will stand in their way* [to accomplish] whatever they decide to do."

Take any two people who have good **communications,** spread them to different corners of the world, and they will eventually come back together and reunite. Nothing will stand in their way!

Conversely, we can extrapolate from this as well: Take any two people who *don't have good* **communications** and put them right **next to each other** – and they will eventually spread to opposite corners of the world.

Open lines of communication, each and every day, are truly a *necessity* toward achieving the goal of Shalom Bayis.

Proper communication is an almost certain remedy for almost any problem.

Contrary to the general idea that problems can get better by just ignoring them, in reality they only become worse. Covering over any misunderstanding rather than fully talking about it and defining it, does not erase the problem; rather, it works as a "springboard" to aggravate it even more. This leads afterward to the eventual resurfacing of the same issue again in a very undesirable fashion, called an "outburst".

> We are only human. At times we may get angry. A set time each day for *calm communication* is an indispensable tool for bridging the gaps when they arise[101].

---

101 Here are a number of worthwhile suggestions to help maintain positivity during any communication time which are presented by Rabbi Simcha Cohen:

1. For the listener: Avoid posing questions or adding non-supportive comments when the talker is still in the middle.
2. Avoid adding grammatical corrections when the talker is still in the middle.
3. For the talker: Avoid speaking in a dictative tone.
4. Avoid speaking in a loud tone the entire time.
5. Avoid speaking very fast.
6. Avoid explaining one point over again a number of times like a kindergarten teacher.
7. Know when to stop speaking. (Habayis Hayehudi, Part 1, pgs. 194–195)

Chapter 15

Daily Communications

From day one, make sure that you have a set time
every single day to speak together [102].

> During that time difficult or sensitive situations can
> be discussed objectively and calmly, allowing both
> of you to define the differences – if not actually to
> touch upon some solutions.

During the rest of the day, if a misunderstanding
should arise, try to control any type of flared

---

102 A practical way of doing this is to decide upon at least one meal a day (breakfast, lunch or supper) that a couple will set for themselves to eat together ("no matter what"), and after the meal issues can be discussed. Rabbi Simcha Cohen adds a number of additional words of advice in planning the set time: 1. Set a finishing time for how long the conversation time will last. 2. Set the time adjacent to a consistent daily event, e.g. after supper, before going to bed, etc. 3. Decide beforehand who will be the "initiator" – the one spouse who will "invite" the other – to the conversation (Habayis Hayehudi, part 1, p. 204).

reaction. Instead, spend the time later that day to organize your thoughts and feelings, to be prepared to present them in a calm fashion during your next *set time* together[103].

> By facing any given issue and fully defining it, a couple is placing a strong investment in their future Shalom Bayis.

As a result of their being able to understand the source of their difference of opinion (and that each of their opinions is ***unintended personally*** at either of them), they will be able to better understand each other in the future and to eliminate any underlying tensions that may have arisen.

> Often a misunderstanding can arise as a result of the natural differences that exist between men and women in their perception of any situation[104]. By taking out the time to define the differences of opinion – in a calm setting where each spouse has the ability to express

---

103 Always be careful not to "force" a conversation when it's not the right time, i.e. when one spouse just walked in or is about to leave; when one spouse is very tired and just wants to go to sleep; some spouses are uncomfortable to speak calmly when riding on a bus. "Forcing" a conversation at such times will likely cause an opposite result to the good feel and closeness that the initiator is really trying to create (Habayis Hayehudi, Part 1, p. 202).

104 See Chapters 6 and 7.

and describe their personal point of view and where they're coming from – a great deal of understanding can be gained for each other, which in turn can result in dissipating the heat of a disagreement – *even if no actual solution to the issue at hand was reached.*

Example 1: Shlomo and Yehudis were in their first year of marriage and were planning a trip overseas for ten days. In the course of their scheduling, they found that one of the locations they would need to stop at for three nights in a row, was in the same neighborhood as Yehudis's parents. Although Shlomo readily agreed to sleep at his in-law's home for *one* night, he was very reluctant to remain there for any additional nights. He was adamant that they should rent a place somewhere else in the neighborhood for the other two nights – even if it meant dipping into their limited savings. Yehudis felt that there was nothing wrong with sleeping at her parents' house for all three nights; especially considering that her parents had offered them the use of the special guest room. When the topic initially arose the discussion became heated, and each spouse felt that the other one's opinion was a personal affront.

By taking out calm time to discuss the issue, it became

clear that the reason that Shlomo felt the way he did, had nothing to do with Yehudis's parents or their home (and certainly not with Yehudis herself). It was just that Yehudis's "baby sister" (now 14), had a habit to check for her "lost items" in the guest room – even when guests were there. This behavior understandably caused Shlomo to feel very uncomfortable.

Once the reason for Shlomo's view was clarified, Yehudis didn't perceive her husband's viewpoint as being aimed personally against her or her family. The fact that the couple had discussed the issue calmly and were able to determine where each of them was "coming from", helped them to be able to understand each other and to remove the feelings of "personal attack" that had arisen from their disagreement. Although even after the discussion the couple still needed to comprise and find an actual *technical* solution for their situation, just the fact that they had *fully defined their differences* served to relieve the major tensions that had developed between them.

Example 2: While guests were visiting and enjoying conversation at Avi and Sarah's home, one of them commented that one side of a bookshelf – that was mounted on the wall by Avi – was slightly lower than the other. Sarah quickly replied: "Well, you know Avi; he's not a professional".

Sarah's inadvertent comment hurt Avi deeply; he had always prided himself on his carpentry and would spend hours developing this ability during his free time. Now Sarah, his own wife, was expressing how she did not value whatsoever any of his accomplishments – even when he performed them with a sincere desire to beautify their home.

The more he thought into it, the more Avi became enraged. His mind had drifted away from the conversation in the room; now, all he felt like doing was to call his wife into the other room and to tell her how he *really* felt – guests or no guests.

By controlling his initial reaction and calming down, Avi gained the benefit of not exploding over an unintended misunderstanding and causing a temporarily severance of his Shalom Bayis. When it came the time for their next discussion together – breakfast of the next morning – Avi raised the issue again calmly, pointing out to his wife that her comment was very hurtful to him.

Sarah was shocked; she hadn't dreamt that Avi would ever take her comment in that way. The reason she had said it, she explained, was because she was actually trying to protect the value of Avi's work from the comment of the guest. What she meant to say, was that Avi is not a professional who works at carpentry full-time, and so even if there is a slight discrepancy, it should still be considered as being perfect. Avi realized that he had misunderstood his wife's intent and had even "mistranslated" her words. It now became apparent that Sarah's intent was totally opposite to what Avi had understood: she was *on* his side, not *against* him. This made Avi realize how much his wife was actually supportive of his accomplishments, rather than thinking how much she is not supportive of him or indifferent.

By initially restraining oneself from having any sort of flared reaction, and by using the calm time to define any issues that may have arisen during the course of that day, a couple can avoid much tension that is often generated by statements or actions that were misperceived.

Two Common Mistakes – To Speak or Not to Speak

There are two opposite miscalculations that are commonly made when utilizing this tool of a "set time" together:

The first mistake is when a spouse is *not able* to

control his initial flared reaction. This leads him to the expression of an extreme reaction that is high-charged emotionally, when it would really have been much more beneficial for him to remain silent. Because of its extremity, a highly-charged emotional reaction will not generate any positive feelings and is likely to be regretted shortly afterwards when things calm down.

> The second mistake, although it may *seem* to be not as severe, is really just as damaging in the long-term. It is the mistake of a spouse **not** speaking and **not** making **any** mention of the misunderstanding when **it is** the time to speak – during the couple's next set time to speak together. Many spouses, who are initially successful at controlling their immediate reactions, tend to feel at the time of their next calm time together: "*Things are going so well right now, why disrupt them by bringing up the disagreement again?*" But this is a mistake.

The point of controlling one's initial flared reaction is not that the misunderstanding should be *ignored*; rather, the point is to gain the opportunity to deal with the issue later on in a non-stressed way. Therefore, when the calm time arrives, the proper thing *to do* is to face the issue and to deliberately bring it up – even though it might feel like the present "positive atmosphere" was disrupted[105].

The Importance of Facing the Disagreement and Defining Its Source

Once an issue has arisen between a couple that has aroused strong emotion, it is indicative of there being underlying differences of view that need to be dealt with. The disagreement can be likened to a sense of pain in the body, which acts as an "alarm system" to make a person aware that he has some underlying physical ailment that needs to be tended to. Ignoring the pain is of no real help, because in the long term the source of pain will only continue to get worse

---

105 Something similar to this issue is not asking explicitly for something when it is a *need*. Very often one spouse does not want to ruin the good feel in the home, nor does he/she want to feel that they are needy to receive something from their spouse – even though they really do *need* it. It is important during the calm time together to voice such requests explicitly rather than just hinting to the request (Habayis Hayehudi, Part 1, p. 307). When the request is voiced explicitly, although it might not feel so good at the first moment to be needy, but at least in regard to communications you know that your spouse has heard the request. If once the request was heard, fulfilling it becomes an issue, than that should be further clarified by the couple just like any other issue that they clarify in their time together. However, *not saying the request clearly* but just *hinting* to it, can very often result in the listening spouse not having "heard" the request at all, which causes the requesting spouse who thought that their request was explicit, to go away from the conversation feeling ignored and distanced.

and worse until it is treated, and only then can it truly begin to heal. Similar to physical pain, to ignore any hurt or upset feeling that a spouse experienced as a result of a disagreement, will not help either of them. The source-cause of their disagreement will most likely continue to fester and to intensify and then will re-surface once again in the not-to-distant future, probably in an even more intense fashion than it appeared the first time.

> Therefore, when using the tool of communication to achieve Shalom Bayis, it is necessary to work in two opposite directions: Initially, at the time of the misunderstanding to try and control any type of flared reaction and to **not say** anything; but then **afterwards**, during the calm time, it is necessary to **yes say** what you felt because of the misunderstanding.

The "pay-off" for a couple who consistently deals with issues that have arisen amongst them, is that once a specific issue was worked out, it will most likely never surface again with the same intensity that it arose with initially. This is due to the fact that once the couple has risen to the challenge and clarified the source reason that was the cause for the heated feelings to arise, the "charge" of that issue was already dissipated.

Chapter 16

Strong Misunderstandings

In extremely emotional situations where you feel you just can't control your reaction, it is actually better to express your feelings to your partner *as soon as possible.* If a strong misunderstanding has taken place to the point where one (or both) of you *are unable to proceed regularly throughout your day, the sooner* you discuss it the better.

> Whenever a strong misunderstanding has occurred, it is very, very important to communicate **as soon as possible** to your spouse that you desire to discuss and define the differences during the next window of time you will spend together. Even if it is technically not possible for you to meet immediately, it is still necessary that you communicate to your spouse that *you **want to discuss*** and deal with the issue *as soon as possible.*

Example: Leah commented to Shimon as he was leaving for the day, "Why don't you ever take a Gemara with you? That way you could at least learn something during your time on the bus." Shimon was extremely offended. He yelled back as he placed one foot out the door: "You are not my *Mashgiach!* You are always judging whether I'm learning or not. As a matter of fact, you always judge me about everything!" Shimon sprinted directly onto the minivan that was waiting to take him. As he sat down, he felt terrible about what had just happened. Leah probably didn't even mean anything by her comment; it just happened to set off something deep *inside of him*. But there was nothing he could do now. He was on a bus hurrying to its destination forty-five minutes away.

> Once Shimon arrived at his job, he just couldn't get started. He made himself something to drink, and then sat down, sulking at his desk. All he could think of was how much he had hurt his wife Leah.

At home, Leah also found it very hard to get started with her housework. She didn't even feel like calling any of her friends. All she could think about was the explosive reaction of Shimon in the morning. She couldn't figure out where this was coming from in him, and she felt very misunderstood.

At his desk, Shimon soon realized that this was a situation of "a strong misunderstanding". He knew that the longer he would leave this without speaking about it, the worse it would get. But what could he do? He had an important meeting that was scheduled to take place in less than five minutes – he couldn't just leave everything now and go home to speak to his wife.

Shimon did the right thing. He immediately opened his phone contacts and called "Home". "Leah", he said, "I'm calling just to tell you that I feel terrible about what happened this morning. I wish I could come home this minute and speak to you all about it – so that we can get to the bottom of this and that it should never happen again; but you know that I have this very important meeting scheduled exactly for this morning. I just wanted to let you know, that I am thinking about you and I don't want to ever again do anything that will hurt you. I will come home as soon as I can, and when I get home we'll talk about this together right away".

By "breaking the ice" of silence that followed the strong misunderstanding, both Shimon and Leah were then able to continue normally throughout their day. Although nothing regarding the actual issue was clarified during the short phone call, Shimon gave the message to his wife that he was upset about the distance between them. He also gave his wife the message that it is of major importance for him to speak with her as soon as possible in order to repair the severed connection. Although Shimon was not actually able to get back to his house until much later that day, the fact that he had made the call relieved much of the tension that was caused by the misunderstanding. It also allowed for the situation to begin to heal a little, as opposed to allowing it to continue to fester off the negative thoughts of each spouse that could build up over the course of the entire day.

Whenever a strong misunderstanding has occurred, it is of extreme importance to communicate ***as soon as possible*** that you desire to discuss the issue together with your spouse at the soonest time possible.

Issues that Involve Money

When the issue at hand involves money and the choices of what to do in practice are limited, it is nonetheless important that the couple clarify

amongst themselves that their differences of opinion
are not meant personally toward either of them,
and that maintaining their Shalom Bayis *is much,
much more important to each of them* than how their
limited budget will be spent. This can be done even
through verbal statements to each other.

> Very often the underlying discomfort in dealing
> with money issues is really the fact that a man – who
> is positioned as the one being responsible for the
> financial resources of the family – has a deep *need* to
> feel that his wife is happy and satisfied from him[106].
> When he begins to sense that *as much as he does* to
> supply monetarily for his home (within the realm of
> his realistic ability) is *not valued or appreciated* by his
> wife whatsoever (or is just *not enough* to award her
> satisfaction), he defines it subconsciously as: "*No
> matter what I do, she will **never** be happy with me and
> my efforts*".

This causes him to pull back even on what he *does
do* for the home, and sometimes to view his wife as
trying to "sink" his plans rather than support them.
This subconscious view itself can then cause havoc

---

106 See footnote 85 above.

to all the work that the couple has put into their relationship[107].

To avoid this situation, a few practical tips are presented here for a woman:

1. Try your best to understand your husband's occasional strong reaction to your requests when he feels he doesn't have enough to fill them . Try to understand his requests in regard to conserving in any area of spending. Realize that his emotional intensity is not coming because he is upset at your requests but rather because he is upset at the limitations *of his own abilities* to fill them.

2. Try to develop those skills of communication which will help you to present to your husband what you're feeling in a way that will not offend him. (See Chapter 15 for advice as to how to lead communications in a way that will bring you closer toward a mutual understanding of each other *rather than to an outburst.* See also Chapter 13:2 as to how to widen your perspective of how you view your husband - by practicing to place the emphasis on your husband's *positive traits* rather than focusing just on

---

107 Habayis Hayehudi, Part 2, pgs.193–194.

his *limitations* (which then opens the path for you to make him feel good about what he *can* do for you and in turn brings him to want to do *even more*) – because this is also an essential tool *to help avoid an outburst* or any type of undesirable expression of feelings.)

3. Be very cautious *never* to say: "So I will buy it from the money *I* made". (This applies to a man as well: Even when he is feeling weak and vulnerable in his position as breadwinner of the family, he should *never* say: "Well, it's *my* money"). Although money that was given to you by an outside source may rightfully be yours, never mention your bank account as being "divorced" from the general needs of the family. This only tends to create distance and wreaks destruction upon the work of building together in partnership[108].

---

108 Habayis Hayehudi, Part 2, p.199.

Chapter 17

The Most Essential Element in Marriage: Trust

When discussing "Communications" in marriage, what is often even more important than *what you say*, is *how you say it*. Even if you are "nice" and "accommodating" to your spouse by always saying the right things, the *tone* with which you say something and which reflects *what you really feel,* can have a greater effect on your spouse than the words you actually say.

> The underlying *feel* that needs to accompany a healthy marriage is **"Trust"**. The feeling of trust between two spouses is the foundation that the entire *marriage rests upon.*

The most important ingredient in the building of a home is "Trust". Some contend that it is "Love", but this is not true. The essence of a marriage is built upon "*trust*": If there is a foundational level of real *trust,* then even if many misunderstandings arise, the couple will likely be able to work them through. However, if there is *no trust,* even if the couple try technically to piece their relationship together, the *deep bond* which is necessary for holding the marriage together for the long-term is not there[109].

In terms of communications, we must be very cautious never to mar this pristine element of the relationship by pronouncing a lie or by denying the existence of a reality without **any** element of truth to our words.

We are *never* permitted to **lie**. Specifically in the case of Shalom Bayis, Chazal have permitted to "*change*" – but never to **lie**. A person may "*change*" – be "*mishaneh*"[110] – when he feels that his partner might not properly understand his intent, but he may never **lie**.

---

109 This may be one reason that can help us better understand the unique Jewish custom to wish a newly married couple that they merit to build a "*Bayis Ne'eman*" – a home filled with *trust* – rather than wishing them the benefits of any other quality. It is "Trust", specifically, that will provide the basis for a home that is strongly bond together.

110 The wording of Chazal is "*Muttar L'shanos mipnei Hashalom*", which is translated as "It is permitted to **change**", not "It is permitted to lie" as is commonly cited. See footnote 112.

In addition to temporarily having severed communications, a lie also causes much more extensive damage to the building of Shalom Bayis: It violates the element of "*Trust*" – the most necessary component in the building of a healthy marriage.

The loss of committing a violation of *trust* cannot be underestimated.

When trust is violated, even once, it will take a long time to rebuild, and even then it is uncertain whether it will ever be able to resume the same level that it was at before the violation.

If at some point in the marriage the component of "*Trust*" was violated, it must be rebuilt. The way to rebuild *trust* is by each spouse actively proving to each other that from now on, *no matter what* the situation may be or whoever is involved, they regard the unity of their marriage as being of *the highest priority* for them; they place the sanctity of their connection to each other above any other person or value that exists [111] (except for Hashem, Whom they are both responsible to above all).

Only through building *trust* can a proper home

---

111 See Chapter 13.

be built. As a couple spends more and more time together over the years, the level of *trust* will also mature and will continue to grow always deeper and deeper.

The "Reset Button" – Belief

Once *trust* was violated, it cannot begin to be rebuilt without first meeting one condition: The couple must be able to *maintain their belief* in the fact that the relationship *can* be rebuilt. Each spouse must first find it in their heart **to believe that it is possible once again to rebuild** and to once again reach full *trust* of each other. Without first finding the place in their hearts to allow for the *possibility of renewed trust* in the future, there is no foundation to build upon.

The Damage Caused by a Lie

If one ever lies to their spouse, it causes a big "crack" in the "bedrock" of *trust*. This is because as much as one would like to believe their spouse and trust them, the overt lie has now caused them to subconsciously question *everything* that their spouse says or does. Since it has become apparent that he or she does not have a problem to place another value above their relationship, it always becomes a question from then on as to whether he or she is repeating the previous behavior and placing another person or value above their relationship. There is very little that can change this suspicion, because the he or she who lied is no longer "trustworthy".

Therefore, we are never permitted to **lie**.

The wording of Chazal telling us that a person can be lenient and "not say everything" for the sake of Shalom Bayis is: "*Mutar lo l'odom **l'shanos** b'dvar haShalom*" – It is permitted to "*change*" for the sake of Shalom (Yevamos 65b). As we know, it is very important to be exacting in the words that Chazal use. They did not say "Mutar *l'shaker*" ("It is permitted to lie"); rather "Mutar *l'shanos*" ("It is permitted to change")[112].

The Difference between "Changing" and Lying

One of the examples that the Gemara brings to illustrate this *halachah,* is in itself an indication as to what Chazal meant when they said "*mutar l'shanos*". The example quoted is the wording that was used by

---

112 I heard this *diyuk* (insight based on the *exact* words that were used by Chazal) in the name of by Rabbi Avraham Blumenkrantz *z"l* from a shiur that he gave on this topic.

Hashem when relating to Avraham Avinu the words
that Sarah had spoken about him.

> Hashem said to Avraham, "Why did Sarah laugh,
> saying, 'Is it even true that I shall give birth though **I**
> have become old'? "[113]. In reality Sarah had said: "And
> **my master** (Avraham) has become old"[114]. Hashem
> "changed" the words of Sarah from having referred
> to Avraham as becoming too old to bear children,
> to that of referring to herself as becoming too old
> to bear children. This change was made, because
> if Avraham would have been told the *exact* words
> of Sarah, it might have caused a rift in the Shalom
> between them.

This example reveals to us the Gemara's intent in its
original statement. **When there is an underlying
reason that one spouse will not be able to relate in
the proper proportion to the words or actions of
the other spouse, yet he still needs to know about
the essence of its taking place, it is permissible to
misrepresent the details – *but only in a way that
still embodies some truth.*** In the case of Avraham and
Sarah, because we know that on a spiritual level the

---

113 Breishis 18 – 13.
114 Ibid, 18 – 12.

two people who marry are really one, it was only a "change" from the statement that Sarah pronounced "and *my master* has become old" to "and *I* have become old". It still embodied an aspect of truth because spiritually both of them were really one *neshama*. It was a "change" from the way the situation is perceived by us in our superficial reality, but on a deeper level it was true. A lie, on the other hand, cannot be construed in any way as being true.

Never Underestimate the Element of Trust

The plus of never lying but rather only "changing", is extremely necessary for maintaining Shalom Bayis: while a lie violates the imperative quality of *trust*, a "change" does not. Even if the spouse who received the "changed" information were to discover the exact truth, it would subsequently emerge from the conversation of the couple that the spouse who "changed" *did not actually lie*. Although they may have described certain particulars of the incident differently than their superficial reality, the words were uttered with a clear intent to maintain *some element of truth*[115]. In a deep subconscious way, this

---

115 Rashi, as well, emphasizes in Parshas Toldos in regard to Yaakov Avinu's

"change" – and even the discovery of it being inexact – actually serves to *further* the level of trust between the couple. The spouse who received the "changed" information now sees, that even when it seemed to their spouse that everything was "hidden", *they would never actually lie* about the essence of an incident if it would bear no resemblance to the truth at all[115a].

> Only through building *trust* can a proper home be built. Although for the sake of Shalom Bayis we may exclude giving full information or the full explanation for our actions, we may never lie. The element of "Trust" must remain *unscathed* in order to properly build a healthy marriage relationship that will last for the long-term. As a couple spends more and more time together over the years, their level of trust for each other will also mature and will only continue to grow always deeper and deeper between them.

____

statement to Yitzchak: "I am – (pause) [Yaakov who has brought you the delicacies; and] Esav is – your firstborn" (Breishis 27:19). Even when Yaakov Avinu was commanded to lie to receive the brachos, he only used his words in a way that would maintain some element of truth to them – so that he would *never* lie explicitly.
115a See also *pasuk* in Bereishis 20:12.

Chapter 18

Pressured Moments

As we discuss healthy communications and avoiding misunderstandings, it is very important to note that very often an angry or heated reaction may be the result of an *external* situation or pressure.

Some examples of *external situations* that can lead to misunderstandings are:
1. Having missed eating a meal;
2. Having missed out on sleep;
3. Trying to leave on time;
4. A hard day at work;
5. A relative who is visiting;
6. When changing apartments;
7. Erev Shabbos.

It is important that both partners be clearly aware, that a misunderstanding which has arisen as result of an *external pressure* is not to be viewed as an indication of their relationship in general. Since the cause of the disagreement is really unconnected to their actual relationship, it is clear that it cannot be taken by either of them as being indicative of the true state of their relationship.

> Sometimes, even shortly after marriage, a misunderstanding can arise due to heightened tensions caused by *numerous* external causes, such as moving apartments, irregular hours of sleep, relatives who are visiting, etc. It is very easy for a couple to start to think, "*Maybe since we can't get along, this has been a mistake and we're really not for each other*".

In truth, however, since it is the *external situation surrounding them* which is the cause of their disagreement, it has no real bearing on their relationship in general. Barring the external pressure – which itself is only temporary – their communications and understanding of each other is really fine.

> It is therefore important for every couple to be aware of these common *external pressures* that are often cause for a misunderstanding.

1. Having missed out on eating a meal.
> It is natural for you to have less patience and to

become more irritable when you have not eaten for a long time. If your spouse has not eaten for a long time or has missed eating a meal, it is probably better not to discuss touchy issues with them until after they have eaten.

2. Having missed out on sleep.

It is very common among young couples to sometimes go to sleep unusually late due to an *external* reason, for example, having attended a Sheva Brochos or a friend's wedding, or having come home late from parent's house, etc. Naturally, the couple then expects themselves in the morning to get up at the same time as they do every morning. By the time the next evening comes around, the exhaustion starts to hit them and it is understandable that both spouses may be feeling quite exhausted. If a misunderstanding should arise between them at that time, it should be clear to both parties that it was *the lack of sleep* that contributed to the misunderstanding – even if the couple claims that they didn't notice being tired at all[116].

---

116 "One of the [main] things that is cause for an uncomfortable feeling to accept a spouse and to be more open to his requests, is tiredness. In our times, women often work outside of their house in addition to their difficult jobs inside the home; this situation can [easily] bring to a "down" in their mood. It is not uncommon when

3. Trying to leave on time.

The pressure that is created by having to get to somewhere on time is something that every couple experiences. If there is a situation where one or both spouses are hurrying to get to a certain destination, especially if monetary loss is involved (e.g. a car service is waiting outside and honking, or if it is necessary for one spouse to rush to get to work

---

a husband comes back home to meet a wife who is angry-faced and tense. Many complaints are heard from men who have revealed that they [feel they] are married to a woman who is "tied down" to [her] work in the house, when they were expecting to be greeted with a smiling face. On the other hand, the wife [generally] does not understand her husband at all, how can he still expect to receive a smile and a shining face after all of her difficult work and toil in organizing the house and in taking care of the children. In addition, many women say to themselves: "If my husband would only feel *a little* of the load that rests upon me, [and] he would offer a helping hand, *then* I would be able to be calmer and to show him a smiling face".

It is appropriate that a woman do as much as she can to rest sometime in the afternoon in order that she have the ability to receive her husband with a smiling face and not hurt his expectations; there will then be a [much] better chance that he will relate to her affectionately and will listen to her requests that he offer a helping hand. Grasping this mind-set [of the husbands'] is very difficult for women and [generally] they do not understand *at all* what is being asked of them; because *it is obvious* that they would prefer to work less [and to rest] and relate to their husband in a more affectionate manner – just that it is not possible for them to let go of taking care of the house and the children. Even so, if it were clear to them without question that their [manner of] relating to a spouse is more important than the care of the house, *then they would* discover the possibility [for them] to push off certain things that need care in the house – and sometimes even to forgo completely (be *mevater*) from doing them – and instead of that, to relate in a positive manner to their spouse" (Habayis Hayehudi, Part 2, p. 312).

or to school), it should be clear to both partners that whatever was uttered under such extenuating circumstances should not be taken as any indication as to how each partner really feels about the other in general.

4. A hard day at work.

If someone makes you upset during the day – especially if it is someone "higher in command", e.g. a teacher, boss, manager etc. – it is very common to just "swallow hard" at the time, and then to feel all the frustration afterwards when coming home. Somehow, *exactly* on those days when we are the most upset because of things that went on *outside* of the home, the most sensitive and touchy issues come up for discussion. This can easily lead to a release of all the previously pent-up frustrations – which are *really* connected to what took place *outside the home* – to then burst forth *inside the home.* The topic of discussion acted only as a "trigger" to bring out the frustrated reaction to what had already happened earlier that day.

It is therefore advisable that you be in touch with what you are feeling throughout the day, and if an upsetting incident has arisen – even one that seemingly has no connection whatsoever to your life at home – you should make sure to mention it to your spouse as soon as possible. By doing so, both of you will now be "on the same page". This is a much better option than to carry around the pain and to act as if everything is fine, because afterwards the hidden pain can very easily be triggered and become a reason for an emotionally heated reaction to burst out at home.

5. A relative who is visiting.

Very often newlywed couples feel – from the goodness of their heart – that it is good to have friends or relatives sleep over in their apartment (which is usually small) – even for an extended period of time. On the one hand this is certainly an act of great *G'milus Chesed;* on the other hand, the reality of having someone else in their apartment places *tremendous* subconscious pressure on the couple.

Many couples do not even realize the extent of this pressure, until it bursts forth in some misunderstanding that has risen between them. The real source of the pressure is very often because one or both of the spouses feel they need to follow certain rules of etiquette or behavior patterns when there is a guest in their home. Often, they may even come to ignore their *own* needs in order to accommodate the guest.

> Every couple – especially one that is newly married – needs their privacy; when someone else is present in the house it *changes tremendously* the dynamic of their home. This is true *especially* in regard to the couple's sense of privacy – even if they deny it and each spouse claims that everything is "fine" for them. Therefore, having guests over for a prolonged amount of time can be *very* detrimental.

In a situation where a couple has no choice and they must have someone sleep over at their home, from my experience with students, for the sake of Shalom Bayis, it is important that a guest sleep over for *no longer than three nights* in a row[117].

6. When changing apartments.

> Whenever moving, no matter how small the move

---

117 In a case where there was absolutely no choice but to have the visiting relative sleep over for an entire week (i.e. the relative came to visit from outside of the country and had no other relatives whatsoever in the place he was visiting other than his children), I have told the student that he could have the relative sleep over for the first three nights, then he should ask the relative kindly to rent a hotel room or some inexpensive lodging for the fourth night, and then the relative could come back to sleep at their house for another three nights in a row.

may seem, the dragging, organizing, packaging, insulating, coordinating with others, etc. are all mentally and physically taxing. The entire moving period, whether it lasts for a few days or a few weeks, should be understood by both spouses as a stressful time that can easily cause misunderstandings to arise. All misunderstandings that arise during that time are very likely to be connected to the stress that has built up from the exhaustion of the move – and are therefore no indication as to the couple's relationship in general. Also included in this category is exhaustion that takes place when *traveling*, as well as all of the days that it takes to prepare *before* the trip and all of the days that it takes to *"recover"* afterwards.

7. Erev Shabbos.

It is **clear** from the Gemara, that Erev Shabbos right before Shabbos is an opportune time for the *yetzer harah* to "visit" a person's home and to cause dissension. The Gemara tells us[118] about Rabbi Meir, who noticed that there was a couple in his neighborhood who would get into arguments every Erev Shabbos. Rabbi Meir made sure to visit the couple's home for three consecutive weeks

---

118 Gittin 52a.

right before Shabbos, in order to mediate peaceful discussion between the couple. Once three weeks went by and the *yetzer harah* was unsuccessful, Rabbi Meir perceived in a spiritual way, that the "negative energy" of the *yetzer harah* had left the couple's home[119].

On the simple level, it is clear why the *yetzer harah* has the ability to cause conflict especially on Erev Shabbos more than at any other time during the week. Shabbos is a time when we need to have already completed all of our weekly chores. This causes a subtle pressure within each person to try and complete everything on time – a pressure that continues to build with each approaching minute of Shabbos. Right before Shabbos, when a person suddenly realizes how much he would still like to do, but how little time he has left to do it, he becomes the most vulnerable to become irritated or upset. Even the mention of one additional responsibility that is incumbent upon him may very well trigger an unexpected outburst[120].

---

119 Rashi, ibid.

120 The Gemara in Shabbos (31a), when describing the unique level of humility that Hillel Hazaken had attained, cites an incident that took place specifically on Erev

Once we are aware of this physical and spiritual
"crunch time" before Shabbos, we can plan ahead
and be careful not to engage in long excursions or
undertake lengthy projects on a short Erev Shabbos.
And if, *chas v'shalom*, a misunderstanding did actually
arise right before Shabbos, a couple should quickly
realize that it is most likely due to the stress of the pre-
Shabbos preparations and should not view it as a true
indication of their marriage relationship in general.

Without a doubt, however, the responsible partner
should certainly make it their priority to apologize
and to ask for forgiveness *as soon as possible* – even
before the Shabbos enters [121].

By being aware of certain *external* situations that can
be cause for misunderstandings to arise, we can try
to avoid these situations from arising, or at least try
to avoid discussing deep or touchy issues at those
times. However, if these situations do arise, it should
be clear to each spouse that since the cause of the
disagreement is the external situation, it is not an

Shabbos – while Hillel was in the midst of his preparations for Shabbos – to illustrate
his unusual level of patience and ability not to get angry even during a time of stress.

121 See Bach on the Tur (Orach Chaim, *siman* 280, piece beginning *v'yehai*), who
speaks explicitly about the importance of this.

indication regarding the compatibility of the couple or of their communications in general. Rather, they should view what took place as an unusual circumstance, and try their best to avoid the pressure that can ensue from such situations in the future[122].

122 If any of the above scenarios were to become constants in the marriage (e.g. constantly changing apartments, housing a long-term guest, etc.), it would be advisable for the couple to plan on some direction that will eventually lead them toward extricating themselves from the external pressure, while in the meantime they continue to constantly remind themselves that all disagreements that arise due to the external pressure are not an indication of their relationship in general. Once the external situation will become limited and is time bound, it will be easier for the couple to relate to each other in the positive way that they need to.

Chapter 19

What Never To Say

As we complete discussing this most essential facet of Shalom Bayis – **communications** – it is important to remember that there are certain things that one should just *never* say:

1. *Never* say anything derogatory about your partner's parents (or immediate family).
2. *Never* say you regret marrying your partner.
3. *Never* say how bad you are or that you have never been a successful person.

> By being aware of certain things *never* to say, we can avoid making statements during times of misunderstandings that are prone to cause a rift of emotions that is much greater than we had intended, and which can take a long time to heal afterwards. It is much wiser to be aware of the types of

statements that can cause emotional scars, and then to make sure to avoid them – ***at all times.***

1. ***Never*** **say anything derogatory about your partner's parents (or immediate family).**

It is important to remember that although we believe that the two people who marry are really two halves of one soul, this is but on the *spiritual* level; on the *physical* level, however, the two have had totally different backgrounds and different experiences from the time that they were born until the time they got married. Although their goal in marriage is to reunite and reach the level of their initial spiritual oneness, that takes years of work. At first, right after marriage, each spouse naturally feels more of an affinity and closeness *to those who they grew up with* and who they have interacted with since their childhood. If during the time of a couple *building together* – namely, before one spouse feels closer to the other more than to anyone else in the world – one says something derogatory about the other's immediate family, it can naturally cause an automatic distance between them. The spouse whose family was spoken about is likely to feel that the comment about their close family member is an indication about how their spouse really feels about *them*. This can automatically cause an unspoken rift between the couple that can continue to fester until eventually it develops into an emotional detachment between the couple.

It is therefore important *never* to lose oneself and say anything that is belittling or disparaging in any way toward one's spouse's family members – even during a time of heated discussion[123].

What To Do if Your Spouse says something Derogatory about their Own Family:

It is advisable, therefore, even in a case where one spouse has expressed dissatisfaction to the other about one of their *own* family members, that the other spouse *not agree* with their words. For example, if one spouse expresses to the other: *"My brother is so mean!"* the other spouse should not reply: *"That's right, I felt the same way about him from the first day I met him!"* Rather, he should be understanding of his spouse's **feelings** and *validate them* by saying: "It's terrible that he causes

---

123 It is important to note here the directive of the Gemara (Berachos 10a): "'The wicked *acts* should be eradicated from the world' (Tehillim 103) – **not** the wicked *people*." Even during times of heated discussion or criticism, we must always take care never to defame or criticize the person themselves, only the *acts* that were done (Habayis Hayehudi, Part 1, p.113).

you to feel that way"; but he should never actually say anything derogatory about the brother himself[124].

2. *Never* say you regret marrying your partner.

Realize that once you are actually married, you are to assume with certainty that this is your *zivug* from *Shomayim*, and that whoever Hashem has brought you together with through the events of *hashgachah*, is exactly that specific person in the world who can help *you* best to reach *your* potential and *your* completeness in this world[125]. Although there may be work to face and differences to bridge, each partner should view this as part of their own specific task in the worship of Hashem.

Included in this category is not to say: "Well, why didn't you tell me that *before* we got married?" or "Did you tell that to the *shadchan*?" The underlying implication of these statements is: "If I would have known about this information beforehand, then I wouldn't have chosen to marry you; and therefore

---

124 See previous footnote.

125 This is all assuming that there are no acts of clear abuse that are being perpetrated and that it is not a situation where no reciprocation is being shown to any of your feelings at all. If you suspect that this is the case, then a third party such as an experienced spiritual guide or a qualified therapist should be sought as soon as possible to determine from an objective point of view how is best to proceed. See also Chapter 22.

I regret what has taken place". According to Jewish *hashkafah*, however, this whole viewpoint is really based upon an incorrect premise.

> If the events of *hashgaha pratis* (Specific Divine Providence) have brought you to the stage of actually becoming married – for whatever reason[126] – then we are to assume that **this** spouse really *is* the **right one** from all the people in the world to bring about the greatest level of *tikun* and completeness for you. It is therefore imperative that each spouse be very careful *never* to say anything in conversation to imply that the entire marriage was by mistake.

Also included in this category is never to mention the word "divorce". Certainly at the time when the couple married they had never thought about this word. As long as it is not mentioned, it remains *far*

---

126 See also footnote 96.

The rule mentioned here relates to the usual case of a couple who met and married through being honest to the best of their ability with each other, and then realized after marriage that there are differences to bridge and misunderstandings to work through. This is considered the situation that normally pervades by every couple and it is in this context that the advice here is being offered. In rare cases, where it is suspected that one spouse intentionally concealed from the other basic information prior to marriage, it is advisable that a third impartial party – such as a Halachic authority – be sought, in order to determine the validity or the fallacy of the suspicion.

from their thoughts. The first spouse to mention
the idea brings it to the forefront of their minds as
a real possibility; and that itself can be a cause for
the marriage to take a turn in the wrong direction.
Although it is human nature to cry out in pain when
being hurt, *chas v'shalom*, and sometimes one spouse
may even feel that they need to control their partner
through the threat of an ultimatum[127], nonetheless
a couple who wants to give their marriage the
best chance of it lasting for the long-term, will
exert extreme caution never to mention the word
"divorce", even during a time of heated discussion or
even just as a joke.

3. *Never* **say how bad you are or that you have
never been a successful person.**

>Although sharing heartfelt truths with a spouse
>is of primary importance, be careful not to share
>condescending statements about yourself. Even if
>you have a spouse whom you feel can contain what

---

127 This does not mean to say that there is never a time when the idea of an
ultimatum needs to be used in order to motivate correction of a serious behavioral
problem. Such a step, however, needs to be expedited only with the guidance of a
knowledgable and experienced third party – see footnote 125. What is referred
to here in the text is the idea of using an ultimatum of divorce just as a matter of
speech in the context of a heated misunderstanding – when the real situation of
the couple in general does not really warrant any such step whatsoever.

you have to say and who can even give you strength, only say how difficult *the situation is* – not what a difficult person *you are*[128].

The reason for this is that whenever a person's words are surrounded with an air of negativity – the listener will hear a negative message, even if the intent was only to share the truth and then to seek positivity in the situation. (The same is true in the opposite way: Whenever a person's words are surrounded with an air of positivity – the listener will hear a positive message, even if the actual message was about something negative.) Therefore, even when sharing your difficult experiences with your spouse, never clothe your words with an air of negativity in regard to yourself. It can cause your spouse to develop a subconscious negative perception of you, which only progresses into an internal distance developing between you, not the closeness which is desired in marriage[129].

---

128 If you are feeling that you have repetitive negative thoughts about yourself, which really need to be spoken out and dealt with, it is important not to "use your spouse" as a therapist. Rather, seek an appropriate therapist who you can work through issues with, and then use the conversation with your spouse to receive positive reinforcement during the duration of your work. Share with your spouse your successes and positive breakthroughs (and just a shorter outline of your difficulties), rather than use them as a therapist to actually work through your side of negative experiences.

129 Habayis Hayehudi, Part 2, p.314.

Included under this heading is also not to speak to your spouse in a way that is considered "cheap" or "street slang". Although every Jewish person is certainly careful to refrain from speaking any prohibited words, to speak even such slang that is permissible, takes away tremendously from building the type of home that a couple really wants. The spouse who uses the lowly form of speech is in effect declaring to his partner: "I am not a respectable person. I am only as important as the type of people who speak this dialect". The unspoken statement behind the words, which is a declaration of a lack of self-respect, when entering the heart of one's spouse, is cause for them to develop a subconscious negative perception and to lose tremendous respect for him. This only serves afterwards to bring about distance between the couple, not the closeness which is desired in marriage[130].

In summary, always be careful once you are married never to say such words of negativity that can have *irreversible* effects.

---

130 Habayis Hayehudi, Part 2, pgs. 318–319.

Chapter 20

"Don't Compare!"

An additional type of speech which is included in the
category of what you should be careful *never* to say
is: *"Why can't you just be like so-and-so?"* This includes
any statement that comes under the heading of
"Comparing". Although it may seem like an innocent
statement, comparing yourselves to other couples
can wreak havoc and plant the roots of separation
between you in a deep subconscious way.

> From the day you begin your home together, agree to
> have a rule between you, that in *your home* you *never*
> *compare yourselves* to any other couple.

The person that Hashem has introduced you to
and ultimately united you with, is someone who is
exactly *what* ***you*** *need* in order for ***you*** to reach ***your***
highest level of completeness. Realize that there is

no one in the world who is perfect, and if you cite someone else as an example of proper behavior in one specific area, realize that there are other areas that the other individual has to work on, that your spouse does not. Therefore, citing selected examples from other couples is only futile, and it is best that you have a clear agreement amongst yourselves, *never to compare yourselves* to any other couple.

> Unfortunately, comparing yourselves to others is a natural tendency, especially for a newly-married couple. The desire to compare comes from the fact that the couple who set out to build their home do not yet have any real idea of how their home should look – other than what they have seen by others. Their point of reference for themselves becomes whatever they have experienced at other people's homes. Therefore, when a question regarding conduct in their own home arises, the couple naturally resorts to comparing themselves to others whom they have each chosen to use as an example.

Comparing, however, carries with it numerous negative implications[131], and even worse – it assumes

---

131 One who compares, implicitly relates the message to his spouse that they are not "good enough". In addition, he creates a subconscious pressure upon his

a premise that is really false. **The entire expectation for one's spouse to perform in a way that is similar to *someone else* – is false.**

No Two People Are the Same Nor Are Any Two Couples

We know from Torah sources that there are no two people in the world who are exactly the same[132]. Each and every person has their own unique strengths as well as their own unique weaknesses. Therefore, because each person is different, it follows that each couple is necessarily different as well.

The goal of each and every couple is to locate **their own** unique balance. The ability to reach that balance is acquired over time, by working together to bridge differences when they arise, by using good communication tools, and by developing a true

spouse to now have to perform as well as the person who was cited as an example. He also causes his spouse to feel from now on under constant scrutiny and to feel constantly judged for how they perform. These implications and subconscious pressures, are extremely detrimental to achieving Shalom Bayis.

132 "Their understandings are not similar one to another, (just like) their faces are not similar one to another" (Brachos 58a). From deeper sources it is clear, that each person has their own *Shoresh Neshama* and their own unique kochos and abilities that Hashem has imbued them with innately, as distinct from any other person in the world (See also *Alei Shur, Chelek Alef, Da'as Atzmeinu, Perek Shlishi, pg. 146.*).

mutual understanding of each other. Each spouse dedicates themselves to contribute from their individual strengths to the collective needs of them together as a couple, in a way where they can both adequately meet each other's *real* needs. Over time, when they both know exactly what acts they need to perform for each other in order to properly address all of each other's real needs, they have then reached the point when they have found **their** *balance.* The specific *balance* and the behavior patterns that the couple develops amongst themselves will be **unique** to *them* as a couple, and **will be distinct from any other couple in the world.**

Therefore, to make any comparison of *their own unique balance* as a couple to any other couple in the world is really like trying to compare "apples and oranges" – two different realities. The way that one couple finds their *balance* and works together, cannot be compared in any way to the way that any other couple in the world finds their balance – no matter how similar they may seem.

Practical Advice

Because of this it is advisable that every couple

adopt the practice of not bringing up comparisons to any other couple in the midst of their home.
If a comparison comes up unintentionally within a discussion, it is a good practice to immediately comment: **"Let's remember the rule that we've accepted: We don't compare ourselves to any other couple"** – and then just continue the conversation, i.e. continue to try and bridge the issue at hand without bringing example from any other couples. "What works best *for us* is what counts, not what works best for anyone else in the world."

> By avoiding making comparisons to other couples or individuals, a couple can avoid the negative implications that are hidden within such statements and their harmful effects. All it takes is to be aware of why comparing is so detrimental, and adopting the simple practice in *your* home of *never* comparing yourselves to any other couple.

Chapter 21

What We Should Say

There are certain statements that are actually beneficial toward the building of Shalom Bayis. For the benefit of building together, each spouse should try to train themselves to use these expressions:

1. Any time after you are married and you are speaking with a third person about your spouse, try not to use the words "*he*" or "*she*". Instead, use the words "*my husband*" or "*my wife*".

2. Whenever someone asks you what you are planning to do or how you are going to do it, train yourself to **answer with the word "*We*" rather than using the words "*I*" or "*Me*":** "*We* were planning", or "*We* still need to discuss what *we're* going to do".

3. Make sure to consistently notify your spouse that you love them and validate them, as much as they need to hear it from you – even if it's every single day.

1. Any time after you are married that you speak with a third person about your spouse, try not to use the words "he" or "she". Instead, use the words "my husband" or "my wife".

> Using a third-person pronoun creates a distance between the speaker and the person being spoken about. In marriage, on the contrary, you are trying to minimize the distance between you and your spouse, and you are aiming to develop what more closeness. You want to instill *in your consciousness* the reality that you are now actually married and that this is "your husband" or "your wife", and not relate to them as if they were just another person without any definition or title. Training yourself to use these references in conversation – even though at the beginning it may seem awkward – is a valuable tool to reinforce *to yourself* your present reality, and to build the relationship into a most sacred and exclusive one.

2. Whenever someone asks you what you are planning to do or how you are going to do it, train yourself to answer with the word "*We*": "*We* were planning", or "*We* still need to discuss what *we're* going to do".

Starting to view your life together as one entity is a huge step forward toward building the marriage relationship to the level that you want to build it to. When others ask you in the singular: "Can *you* come to an important meeting on Thursday night?", Or "Can I come over to *your* house for a meal?" The natural tendency from years of having lived as a single person, is to offer an immediate answer based upon your personal considerations alone. But since you are now trying to view your life together with your spouse as both of you being one entity, try to resist the instinctive reaction and answer instead: "Let me check what **we** were planning to do Thursday night", or "I will let you know once **we** talk about it". This gives you and the others around you the sense that you **really are** married, and that the decisions in your life are no longer made by each of you individually, but by the entirety of both of you together.

It is healthy to train yourself to think: There is no "*just me*" anymore.

Sacrificing Unilateral Independence to Gain the Unified Strength of a Couple

Giving up some of your independence in decision

making might feel like a "step down" for you. You
might think: "Initially I was so independent – I could
do *whatever* I wanted *whenever* I wanted and I didn't
have to ask anyone – and now I have to discuss
everything I want to do with my spouse." In reality,
though, it is really a huge step *upward* for you.

> Real greatness, is when a person can grow and
> extend himself to include others and relate to **their**
> needs – whether it be those of a husband/wife,
> children, students, or community[133] – rather than
> to remain perpetually focused on the "ME" – and to
> relate only to those needs which are "my *own* needs".
> Once you are married, you need to train yourself to
> be in the mind-set of constantly practicing to bear
> the responsibilities of life *together* – to *share* in times
> of triumph and in times of disappointment, and to
> *share* in making decisions. The *unified strength that
> you will gain* from doing so, will prove over time –
> with Hashem's help – to be **exponentially greater**

---

133 See *Sefer Alei Shur, Chelek Alef – Sha'ar Revii,* where the aforementioned levels of
marriage, children, students etc. are all described in the form of a progression, each one
being a further level of **inclusion** of others within *one's own* personality (beginning of
Maamar Rishon). The level of a person is revealed through *his sincere interest* in being
focused on using his abilities to help others – starting with those who are closest to him
– rather than it being focused on using his abilities to only fill his own needs.

than anything you have felt in the past. It allows you to begin to feel the inner strength necessary to withstand the pressures of almost any situation in the world, and to emerge from them successfully and admirably.

3. Make sure to consistently notify your spouse that you love them and validate them, as much as they need to hear it from you – even if it's every single day. Every person in the world is searching mainly for two things: Love and Validation[134] . **Every human being's basic needs are constructed in such a way that he must have *love* and *validation* in order to feel satisfied.** The deepest levels of both of these needs are expressed in marriage. Just like a person needs to eat and sleep again each and every day, so too *they need to feel loved and validated from anew – each and every day.*

When a couple have merited a close relationship that has built already over a long time, it may be that it is their practice not to express the love and validation *in words,* since they can already express it through their actions. But the proper way to create positivity in the home is really to make sure to convey this message

____

134 Zohar, *Chelek Alef,* 49a, in explanation of the *pasuk* of Bereishis 2:23.

verbally[135]. Even if there are times when saying the words "I love you" may be inappropriate, one can still tell their spouse how much they value them and their unique G-dly traits, whenever the situation presents itself.

> Everyone in the world has G-dly traits. There is no one in the world who doesn't have any[136]. Sometimes, because of the leanings of society, or the subjective values of mass media, one or another trait does not receive its true objective value. If a person really cares about their spouse, and their main goal in the relationship is to *give* whatever the spouse needs, then they will make it a point to determine and define the gifted traits that they observe which their spouse embodies naturally[137]. They will then focus on those G-dly traits that their spouse is specifically gifted with and they will always respect and give them value for their objective importance, no matter what society says.

Moshe and Chava were married for many years; so many years as a matter of fact, that Moshe's custom

---

135 Habayis Hayehudi, Part 2, p.316.

136 Chovos Halevavos, Sha'ar Habitachon, perek *gimel*; Alei Shur, *Chelek Alef*, p.146.

137 For a tool to help with locating your spouse's natural positive traits, see a list of positive character traits in Appendix 2. Also see Alei Shur, Ibid.

of not acquiring any cellphones in their family had become obsolete. Close friends of Chava would sometimes blurt out in shock: "How can anyone live post 2015 without a cellphone?" It was almost as if Moshe's custom, originally adopted for the sake of self-development and *avodas* Hashem, had no place of existence in the present reality of society. Nonetheless, Chava was careful to give importance to her husband's *temimus* (wholehearted unquestioning behavior) and his sincere, wholehearted connection to Hashem – even when it came with the cost of dislocating from much of the present day society. She would mention to him her respect of his dedication to Hashem daily, and she would make it a point to praise among her friends her husband's quality of rescinding from the distractions of this world for the sake of growing spiritually – even though in regard to the present-day society such behavior was not viewed as praiseworthy.

In truth, Moshe and Chava's connection, when built with such expression of ongoing validation and love, was really *stronger* than any of the subjective values that the society was "selling" – even though it may seem to us on the external level that they remained living on a very "low-progressive" stance in post-2015 society.

For the purpose of achieving your goal in marriage, and for the purpose of building that strongest bond which can withstand any of the transient changes and crazes of society – remember to reinforce verbally your validation and love for your spouse as much as they need to hear it.

Chapter 22

Real Source Problems

By being aware of certain intrinsic differences that exist between every man and woman, and by keeping open and healthy communication lines, we now have B'ezras Hashem valuable tools to bridge the gaps when they surface, and thus to merit the greatest accomplishment of our Torah lives: Shalom Bayis.

> If there ever are any core problems that arise, **chas v'shalom**, make sure to seek advice from *experienced* spiritual and professional guidance sources **what sooner**.

It is also important not to involve too many other people. It is best to receive guidance from **only one or two** other sources. Experience has proven, that the more people there are who are involved, the more place there is for confusion to set in, **chas v'shalom**.

> By seeking guidance *what sooner,* and by *not publicizing* their personal issues and challenges, a couple thus gives themselves the best chance possible to work through their issues – even though they may seem overwhelmingly deep.

Even at times when it may seem close to impossible, if a couple guards their private information appropriately and they gear it only toward those individuals *who are equipped to deal with the situation in a discreet and professional way,* they then give themselves the best chance possible to merit the ability to bridge their gaps, and to ultimately achieve for themselves the Shalom Bayis which they truly seek.

Chapter 23

Make Hashem A Partner

As with every aspect in our daily lives, we need to constantly pray and entreat Hashem that we be *zoche* to Shalom Bayis.

> When good communications, real trust, respect and love exist between the couple, the first step toward good chinuch for their children, **im yirtze Hashem**, has already been taken.

If the two people are connected to Hashem and are connected to each other on a real level, there are no stress situations in the world that can shake them.

> This is the marriage which is likened by Chazal to a small "Beis Hamikdash" – to a **Mikdash Me'ot,** which is the necessary precedent to lead us to the building of the real Beis Hamikdash – the home for the unity of feelings between *the entire Jewish nation* and their

All-powerful, All-encompassing, Benevolent and Giving *husband*[138] – *Creator of the World,* Who has individual recognition , validation and love *for each and every one of us* – May it come speedily in our days, Amen.

---

138   Shir Hashirim (3:11). Throughout the entire Shir Hashirim, Shlomo Hamelech compares the relationship of the Jewish nation and Hashem to a couple who are totally united on the levels of thought, emotion, and action. The reason that Shlomo Hamelech compiled this sefer using such a comparison, is because he wanted to give us a point of reference to the authentic relationship between Jewish souls and the Creator by means of our own *parallel experience* of a successful marriage in this world. The experiential knowledge that we gain from working on a positive and truly unified marriage, acts as the greatest point of reference we have for understanding the true relationship of our souls with the Creator. According to the Shulchan Aruch (Orach Chaim 231), this should really be our main intent in the experience of marriage – to know through the experience of the relationship how great is really the level of love and connection that we could feel from Hashem – the Ultimate and True Source of every pleasure and satisfaction that exists in the entire world.

Appendix 1

What to look for in a Shidduch

Since this sefer was compiled with the idea of it being read even before marriage, it is understood that many may read the sefer even before they have begun shidduchim.

As such, I have added an appendix of suggested traits that a person can check for in a prospective shidduch.

- *Yiras Shamayim* (keeping Torah *halachah* even when no one sees)
- Good *middos*
- Physical and mental health[139]
- Flowing communications
- Mutual understanding
- Attraction
- Similar spiritual goals

---

139 The first three criteria on this list were the advice given by the previous Belzer Rebbe, Rebbe Ahron of Belz *z"l*. The rest of the list are additional factors that I have come to notice are important, from my experience with students over the years.

Appendix 2

List of Innate Traits *-* Use as a checklist

Intellectual Traits

- Book-Smart
- Academic
- Wise
- Analytic
- Deep
- Understanding
- Sharp
- Pensive
- Clear-Thinker
- Logical
- Quick-Grasp
- Good Memory
- Insightful
- Thorough

Emotional Traits

- Intuitive
- Life-Smart
- Compassionate
- Genuine
- Sincere
- Truth-Seeking
- Spiritual
- Determined
- Serious
- Truthful
- Loyal
- Devoted
- Deliberate
- Empathetic
- Sensitive
- Gentle

- Caring
- Generous
- Sociable
- Accepting
- Enthusiastic
- Passionate
- Confident
- Courageous
- Assertive
- Just
- Right
- Considerate
- Straight
- Simple
- Modest
- Pure
- Dignified
- Pedant
- Humble
- Patient
- Aesthetic
- Sweet
- Friendly
- Reserved
- Warm
- Open
- Expressive
- Easygoing
- Cheerful
- Tolerant
- Adventurous
- Stable

Action Traits

- Business Sense
- Managerial
- Networker
- Salesman
- Initiator
- Resourceful
- Responsible
- Organized
- Mechanical
- Tech-Savy
- Practical
- Tactful
- Perceptive
- Alert

- Punctual
- Polite
- Meticulous
- Tidy
- Orderly
- Active
- Respectful

Skills and Talents

- Creative
- Artistic
- Precise
- Decorative
- Musical
- Composer
- Dancer
- Singer
- Actor
- Athletic
- Good Coordination
- Flexibility
- Straightforward
- Self-Control
- To Cook
- To Bake
- To Draw
- Endurance
- Sense of Humor
- Funny
- A Speaker
- Animated
- Brave
- Charm
- Natural Beauty
- Handy
- Artisan
- Adaptive

May the Learning in this sefer be an *I'luy Nishmas* for

Yosef Elimelech
Ben Reuven *a"h*
Stern

Niftar Sivan 20, 5779

He taught us how to be loving and
genuine to ourselves and to others.

He was a personification of the Mishna: Love all
Hashem's creations and bring them close to Torah.

He felt so deeply about everyone
and anyone, and loved them for who they were.

He was always there "in the moment" – not only in the
moment itself – but in the moment "with you".

His smiling and nurturing
presence remain alive with us.

Dedicated by his loving family,

**Rebbetzin Denise, Moshe Chaim and Rachel,
Yossi and Blima, Zack and Devori, Shiya and Elie**

I'lyui Nishmas our dear friend

Mike Stern

Our time spent in Yeshiva was formative
and our love for you enduring.

Even from afar you gave to
our family over the years,
particularly with your steadfast
belief in us and our capabilities.

We miss you!

Michoel and Bruchi Barnett

לעילוי נשמת
My warmest friend and wisest chavrusa

Rabbi Michael Stern

Yosef Elimelech
ben Reuven *z'l*

He lived to give – and I was fortunate to be on the receiving end for almost three decades.

We miss you dearly.
Love always,
Eli Glaser

Elimelech (Mike) Stern

will always be remembered by me, as a former roommate in the *Moshav* dorms at Aish HaTorah, who was larger than life in his אהבת ישראל.

Mike was so full of life and שמחת החיים that one could not help but love him.

May he continue to be remembered by all those whom he touched and may he be a מליץ יושר for his family. We miss him dearly.

Moshe & Dinah Krygier

Mike's approach to bringing people closer, was that
he showed them how much the Almighty *cares about
them* – and *that* brought them closer to Hashem.
First he showed people that *he himself* purely
cared about them, then he would *open his heart* to
them, *then* he would talk to them about G-d.

May that legacy continue to be a lesson for us.

Rabbi Jamie Cowland

Dedicated to a man with a
heart of gold and a soaring spirit.

לעילוי נשמת

Yosef Elimelech
ben Reuven *z'l*

Your legacy lives on.

Nasanel and Rivkah Bergman and family

You were the best friend anyone could hope for; Always there to brighten my day, seeing the best in me without fail, sharing yourself and your wisdom with me and always guiding our relationship towards growth, in that natural, easy-going and optimistic Mike Stern way!

You will be forever in my heart.
Rabbi Simcha Barnett

In memory of man who was truly loved/אהוב by all who knew him.

We feel blessed and grateful to have spent so many years with him.

Mike, we will always miss you.

With love and respect,
Rabbi Yakov & Nili Couzens

Mike,
You were the best friend to everyone you met.

We miss you.

Please be a *meilitz yosher* for us in *shomayim*.

Rabbi David Ordan

In honor of

Yosef Elimelech
ben Reuven *z'l*

A *yedid* to every one of Hashem's children and an extraordinary example of loving kindness, wisdom, and perseverance for good.

Rabbi Chanoch Harris

In honor of my dear brother

Elimelech Stern *z"l,*

He gave his heart and
neshamah for Hashem and
Klal Yisrael.

May his memory be *baruch* -
.יהא זכרו ברוך

Rabbi Chaim Levine

Mike, with his positive energy
and gregariousness,
Inspired everyone to feel
good about himself.

Kindheartedness and caring
Exuded from him.

תנצב"ה

He is deeply missed.

The Kalsmiths

Rabbi Mike brought out the
uniqueness and greatness in
everyone he met.

He loved people for who they
were and taught us all how to
believe in ourselves.

Rabbi David Begoun
Deerfield, Illinois

Rabbi Mike knew that it's
G-d's will to reach out to
others and to guide them to
develop as unique individuals –
each person according to
his own specific qualities.

He saw the Divine Presence –
the intrinsic "image of G-d" –
in every human being.

**Aryeh Leib and Chava
Devorkin**
Milwaukee

In Honor of my good Friend
Mike Stern.

May this book be a *zchus for
your beautiful Neshama.*

Kurt Stein

Dedicated
to the memory
of the amazing life of
Rabbi Mike Stern.

**Rabbi Tzvi and Ruth
Gluckin**

Rabbi Mike was what this
generation needs:

Someone to first see *you,*
to love *you* openly, to truly
care about *you* –
And *then* to bring you
close to G-d.

Daniel Hyman
Treasurer,
Yeshiva Elementary School,
Milwaukee

A beautiful soul.

It was an honor
to know him.

Rabbi Adam Jacobs

Rabbi Mike Stern was my very first chavrusa and introduced
me to the beautiful world of Torah, mitzvos and the
Ner Yisrael Yeshiva community in North Toronto that
we have called home for over 25 years.

He was an example to everyone, to love each other,
to value each other and to be there for each other.

He was a great friend, mentor and neighbor in the Old City
when we studied at Aish HaTorah together.

His impact will never be forgotten.

Mark (Yerucham) Halpern, Toronto, Canada

Special Thanks to
HIDABROOT
for their
support in this effort

www.ingramcontent.com/pod-product-compliance
Lightning Source LLC
Chambersburg PA
CBHW071942150726
47999CB00001B/293